THE MANY LIVES

— OF —

ANDREW YOUNG

A Very Special Thanks

Team ———— *Supporters* ———— *Family*

Team	Supporters	Family
Donald Edward Bermudez	Chick-Fil-A	Carolyn Young
Amanda Brown Olmstead	Delta Air Lines	
Rodney Cook Jr.	The Coca-Cola Company	Andrea Young
CB Hackworth	Arthur M. Blank Family Foundation	Lisa Alston
Gaurav Kumar	Google	Paula Shelton
Paul Rosser	NewSouth Books	Andrew "Bo" Young III
Dr. Ba-Shen T. Welch	Tom Williams	
	Walgreens	

THE MANY LIVES

—— OF ——

ANDREW
YOUNG

Ernie Suggs

Foreword by Jimmy Carter
Introduction by Gaurav Kumar

NewSouth Books
Montgomery

NewSouth Books
105 S. Court Street
Montgomery, AL 36104

PUBLISHER'S CATALOGING-IN-PUBLICATION DATA

Names: Suggs, Ernie, 1967– , author. | Carter, Jimmy, 1924– , writer of foreword.
| Kumar, Gaurav, 1980– , writer of introduction.
Title: The many lives of Andrew Young / Ernie Suggs ; Foreword by Jimmy Carter
and Introduction by Gaurav Kumar. —1st ed.
Description: Montgomery, AL : NewSouth Books, [2022] | Includes index. |
Identifiers: ISBN 9781588384744 (hardback).
Subjects: LCSH: Young, Andrew J., Jr. | United States—civil rights leaders—
members of Congress—ambassadors—mayors—Biography. | African
Americans—New Orleans—Washington—New York—Atlanta—Biography. |
Civil rights—United States—the South—Alabama—Florida—Georgia—voting
rights—nonviolence—History—20th century. Politics and government—United
States—the South—Congress—United Nations—municipalities—20th century.
| Race relations—United States—the South—20th century. | Social culture—
United States—Olympics—poverty—education—health—climate change—food
security—sustainability—20th–21st centuries. |

Design by Donald Edward Bermudez

Printed in Canada by Friesens

*The Black Belt, defined by its dark, rich soil, stretches across central
Alabama. It was the heart of the cotton belt. It was and is a place of great
beauty, of extreme wealth and grinding poverty, of pain and joy. Here we
take our stand, listening to the past, looking to the future.*

PHOTO SOURCES

Our best efforts have been used to obtain proper copyright
clearance and credit for each of the images in this book. If
an unavoidable and inadvertent credit error is discovered,
it will be corrected in future editions. All photographs are
used courtesy of the author unless otherwise noted. Cred-
ited photographs are owned by the photographer and/or
his successor or assign, and may not be reproduced in any
manner. All rights reserved.

END SHEETS: Pattern design, Cornerstone Image (back)

FRONT MATTER: Page 1, Book Title 2 Special Thanks ©
Bud Smith, Page 6 The Atlanta Journal-Constitution, Dwight
Ross Jr., Jimmy Carter Foreword, Page 8, 9 Gaurav Kumar
Introduction, Page 6, Preface Ernie Suggs 10, Spider Martin
(watermark image) 11

CHAPTER 1 EARLY YEARS: Amistad Research Center, Daisy
Fuller Young Papers, Pages 12–15, 17, 18, 28, 29, Andrew
Young Personal Collection Pages 19, 20, 26 CB Hackworth
Archives 22, 23

CHAPTER 2 COLLEGE: Andrew Young Personal Collection
Pages 31, 32, 34, 35

CHAPTER 3 THE PREACHER: Auburn Avenue Research
Library (AARL), Andrew Young Papers, Pages 38, 40 (top
left), 34, 35, 42–46, 48, 56, 63–69 Amistad Research Center, Daisy Fuller Young Papers, 43 (middle images), 50–53,
60, 61, Andrew Young Personal Collection, 49, 54, 55, 58,
62, 70, 71.

CHAPTER 4 AGENTS OF CHANGE: Ernest Withers, 72, 92,
93 (top right) SCLC Archives (left) Spider Martin (right) 73,
88, Auburn Avenue Research Library (AARL), Andrew Young
Papers, Pages 73, 76, 79, 87, 88, 96, 98, 99, 100–103, 107,
108, 110, 111 APimages 74, 83, 86 (bottom), 90 (left), Library
of Congress, 75, 87, (top right) Andrew Young Personal
Collection, 77–79, 82, The State of Florida Archives (middle
images right) University of Georgia Archives, 79, 80, Bjonr
Finstad, 83, © Steve Schapiro and courtesy of Jackson Fine
Art. 84, 85, Spider Martin 86, (top left, left middle) Granger
/Vernon Merritt III pg 87, Charles Moore, Alamay Stock
(right) 89, Joseph Louw 93, (right bottom) © Yousuf Karsh
95, 105, Bob Fitch 101, Johnson Publishing (top right) Elaine
Tomlin 102, Ronald S. Comedy 103, Bob Adelman 96, 97,
Bud Smith 96 (left middle), Dennis Brach 109, (Right)

CHAPTER 5 CONGRESS: Johnson Publishing, Moneta
Sleet, Jr. Pages, 112, 118, 119 (bottom), 132, 133, 140 (top
left), Auburn Avenue Research Library (AARL), Andrew
Young Papers, Pages 113–117, 119–121, 123–125, 130,
131, 134, 136–139 Bill Wood Associates, 126, The Atlanta
Journal-Constitution, 128, Amistad Research Center, Daisy
Fuller Young Papers, Pages 129, (both) 140, Library of Con-
gress 141, 142, Jules Schick 143, Dev O'Neill 144, United
Nations Photo; 145.

CHAPTER 6 THE AMBASSADOR: Library of Congress page
148, 152, 154 Amistad Research Center, Daisy Fuller Young
Papers, Pages 149, 162 (background), 163, 173, United Na-
tions/ Photo By Y. Nagata 166, © Camrapix, Pages 164 (left),
© Keystone Pictures USA/ZUMAPRESS.com Alamy 164 (left
bottom), AP Wirephoto 150, Alamy 151, 153, 160 (AARL),
Andrew Young Papers, 156–158, 166, 168, 169, 171, 172,
CB Hackworth Archives 159, United Nations 161, 163, 166,
167, Dennis Brach 162 (left bottom), Johnson Publishing166
(Bottom Left) Michos Tzovaras Photography 170, JD Scott
174, Carter Presidential Library, Archives, 175.

CHAPTER 7 THE MAYOR: Amistad Research Center, Daisy
Fuller Young Papers, Sue Ross, Carol Muldawer, 177, 176,
Andrew Young personal collection178, 179, Dev O'Neill,
180, Auburn Avenue Research Library (AARL), Andrew
Young Papers, 177, 176, Sue Ross 183, Willie Tucker 187,
Casey Wright, mural artist Lillian Blades, 188, 189

CHAPTER 8 OLYMPICS: Auburn Avenue Research Library
(AARL), Andrew Young Papers, 192–196, 198–208, AJC
(right) 197, 207

CHAPTER 9 THE FOUNDATION: Oliver Danner, 212, 213,
CB Hackworth, Archives Auburn Avenue Research Library
(AARL), 236 (bottom) Andrew Young Papers, Mark Waugh
/Alamy Stock Photo, Andrea Young Collection (left top) 236,
Page 236, 237 Videographers: Scott Auerbach, Mike Chase,
Anthony Daniels Dave Dawson, Dan McCain, Video Editor,
Mark Bryant, Producer, Jane Cole, Director, CB Hackworth,
Executive Producer, Andrew Young 216–227.

CHAPTER 10 THE WORLD TRAVELER: Auburn Avenue
Research Library (AARL), Andrew Young Papers, Photo I.D.
Beri (India), 244–247 Andrew Young Personal collection,
Page 238–243, 248–255 Casey McDaniel Wright 241, 261,
Carol Muldawer 250–257.

CHAPTER 11 FAMILY: The private collection of the Young
Family, Andrea Young, Lisa Alston, Paula Shelton and Andrew
Young III. Casey McDaniel Wright 261.

EPILOGUE: Auburn Avenue Research Library (AARL),
Andrew Young Papers, 262, © Regan Murphy, page 264

ACKNOWLEDGMENTS

We offer our heartfelt thanks to the following organiza-
tion and photographers: Amistad Research Center and staff,
Laura Thomson, MLS, MA, Phillip Cunningham, MLIS, Lisa
C. Moore, MLIS, (Daisy Fuller Young Collection) Auburn
Avenue Research Library, and Staff, Derek Mosely, Kayla
Morris, Okezie Amalaha (Andrew J. Young Papers) Photog-
raphers: The Atlanta Journal-Constitution, Steve Schapiro,
Spider Martin (Tracy Martin), Bud Smith, Casey McDaniel
Wright (for your inkind gifts)

Contents

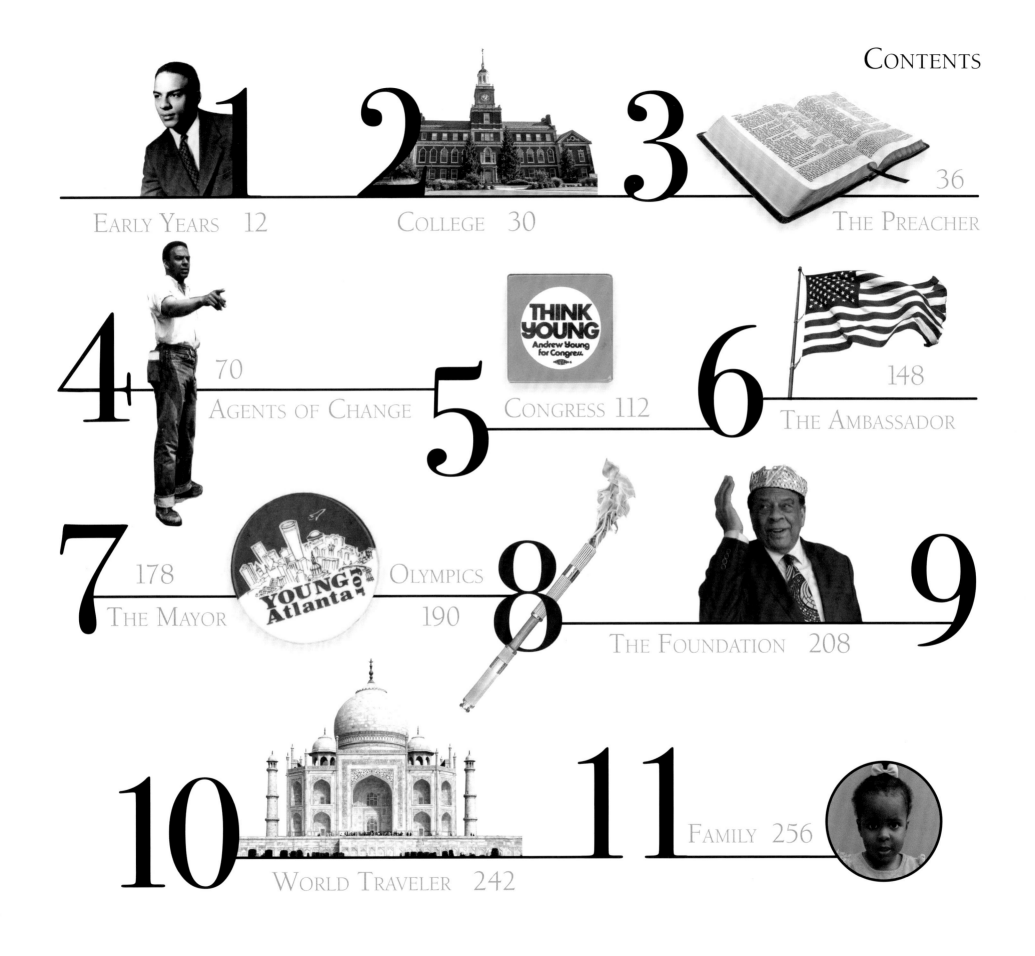

Honoring Andy on his 90ᴛʜ birthday

JIMMY CARTER
39ᴛʜ PRESIDENT OF THE UNITED STATES

When, at the close of my Administration in January 1981 I awarded the Presidential Medal of Freedom to Andrew Young, I cited his lifetime of dedication to human rights. Alongside Martin Luther King Jr., he had risked his life to assure that the rights guaranteed in the United States Constitution belonged equally to all Americans. I had been honored to win his support when I decided to run for President. His vouching for me was crucial to my successful campaign for the Democratic nomination. Once I was elected, I knew that he could strengthen the ties of friendship and respect between our nation and the nations of Africa, Asia, and South America, which was a high priority for me, and I asked him to leave the Congress and serve as our UN Ambassador. He accepted, and he fulfilled my expectations. He was especially important in working to bring equal rights to citizens of Rhodesia and South Africa.

After my presidency, Rosalynn and I decided to continue our public service by launching The Carter Center in Atlanta. Andy, who became the city's mayor, supported me again by helping me secure a site, then covered in kudzu, but with great potential for the future. In the early years of the Center, he served on our Board of Advisors. Later, he participated in our conflict resolution efforts as a member of the International Negotiation Network. Over the years, he always has been there when I needed him. As an articulate and inspiring storyteller, he often has been called to speak about me and for me.

In 2019, Andy came down to Plains to teach Sunday School with me. As I've said before, he speaks from the heart with deep commitment. He speaks out of religious conscience and with a preacher's eloquence. I am not the only one in my family who felt that way. Back in April 1977, my mother told a reporter that Andy "is the only one I listen to. These days, Jimmy is too full of politics." Andy is a great man and a national treasure. I am fortunate that he also is a close and intimate friend. Rosalynn joins me in wishing him a very happy ninetieth birthday.

Introduction

THE MANY LIVES OF ANDREW YOUNG

GAURAV KUMAR

PRESIDENT, THE ANDREW YOUNG FOUNDATION

Gaurav Kumar and Ambassador Andrew Young
Soong Sil University, Seoul, Korea

I met Ambassador Young, a chance encounter, on his 80th birthday on the stairs of the Millennium Gate in Atlanta. He was four steps below me and turned around and said "Young man why don't you go ahead, my knees are bad and I will take time." I looked at him and said "Ambassador, I like to follow leaders. Please go ahead and I will follow you." Within five minutes we were chatting about how to change the world, asked me to work with him on Mobile Harbor project and gave me his cellphone number. This was ten years ago. I get up every morning feeling blessed for having the opportunity to learn from his wisdom, compassion and leadership everyday.

Not many who are born become leaders. Not many who become leaders do good for the people. Not many leaders who do good for the people have the vision for the future generations to thrive. Andrew Young is a living legend who possesses these qualities, and it is important that his life and works are celebrated and preserved in perpetuity to inspire the generations to come. His life is a testimony to an outstanding human achievement in one lifetime, driven by an undaunted faith in God.

In the following pages, author Ernie Suggs takes us on an unforgettable journey through the life of Andrew Young. This is the first literary attempt to cover his entire life. His life is an ocean of peace, and we have tried to capture some of its waves through numerous photographs, anecdotes, and stories told by him personally. The various chapters will resonate with so many of us who have had the blessing to be able to work with this great man.

From an early age in his New Orleans neighborhood, Young learned to find common interests in opposing viewpoints, and consensus-building among the diverse ethnicities in his community. As a nineteen-year-old graduate of Howard University, after a God-present encounter on a mountain, he embarked upon seminary. As a pastor in Georgia, he organized voter registration drives, resulting in his subsequent leadership

Decades that resonate in shaping the world.

role in the Southern Christian Leadership Conference (SCLC). At the SCLC, Young worked with Martin Luther King Jr. and others in teaching nonviolence as a means of gaining full citizenship for blacks.

Mahatma Gandhi followed the principle of nonviolence to free India from British rule. Satyagraha was an innovative method of civil resistance that inspired the civil rights movement in the United States. Nonviolence is deeply rooted in spirituality, and with his background in divinity, Andrew Young was poised to instill this philosophy in his life. His leadership in the movement as a chief strategist and negotiator during its campaigns played a part in the passage of the Civil Rights Act of 1964 and the Voting Rights Act of 1965—changing the course of history of this nation and the world.

It's important to understand that America would not have attracted the global talent to innovate and prosper if there would not have been an end to legal segregation that was achieved in the 1960s.

As the first black Congressman from Georgia since Reconstruction, he served on the banking committee and sponsored legislation that established the United States Institute for Peace, while simultaneously securing federal funds for the Metro Atlanta Rapid Transit Authority (MARTA), a new Atlanta highway system, and the creation of the Chattahoochee National Park.

As the country's first black Ambassador to the United Nations, he helped craft the first U.S./ Africa policy with human rights at its core. He had the hindsight and foresight to understand the geopolitical importance of the continent, whose peoples and population shifts are such that it is now predicted that by 2050, one out of every three persons on the planet will be in Africa. Ambassador Young positioned the United States as an ally and partner with the continent.

He was elected in 1981 as mayor of Atlanta and was reelected in 1985 with more than 80 percent of the vote, pioneering the transformation of Atlanta into an international city. As mayor, he attracted more than 1,000 new businesses, created one million new jobs for the region, brought in $70 billion in foreign direct investment, and championed expansion of the Hartsfield-Jackson Airport, one of the world's busiest airports. While Young was mayor, Atlanta also became the number one convention center in the world. In keeping with his spirit for evangelizing peace and his love for track and field athletics, he led the effort that brought the 1996 Summer Olympic Games to Atlanta. During his tenure as mayor, GA-400, Freedom Parkway, and the Carter Library were built.

In 1996, he co-founded Good Works International to provide specialized insight for emerging markets in Africa and the Caribbean. That work continues with the Andrew J. Young Foundation, founded in 2003, with the mission to feed the hungry, clothe and house the poor, heal the sick, and set at liberty those who are oppressed.

The Foundation is working on social innovations to produce more food on less land, using less water and energy, to sustain the planet and empower people to grow their own food. It is our moral responsibility and duty to ensure that no human being goes to bed hungry. Mother Nature has given us enough resources to feed everyone on this beautiful planet.

As you savor this book and the life it celebrates, we hope it inspires you to partner with our foundation to write a story that is yet incomplete for a world that is in desperate need of our collective efforts and love to effect change in the lives of the least of God's children.

During moments of privacy and transparency, Martin Luther King and Andrew Young lamented that the social justice mission to transform humanity from a place of darkness to a place of light would more than likely take a century. They knew this endeavor would be a relay, not a sprint.

There is more work to be done.

As we honor and celebrate Ambassador Andrew Young's ninetieth birthday, help us continue this work.

There Goes an Alpha Man

ERNIE SUGGS

AUTHOR

I met Andrew Young for the first time in Durham, North Carolina in 1996. I was a young reporter for the Durham Herald-Sun and I was assigned to cover a lecture that he was giving about his new autobiography, *An Easy Burden.*

Having attended a black college, North Carolina Central University, I of course knew and respected Young's legacy, particularly his role as a civil rights leader working alongside Martin Luther King Jr.

But my "introduction" to Young came in the 1970s as a child growing up in Brooklyn. My mother was a huge Jimmy Carter fan, and by extension, so was I. My mother also made an effort to guide me toward the works of exemplary blacks. So I learned all I could about the country's first black United Nations ambassador, who had earlier become the first African American to represent Georgia in Congress since Reconstruction and later the mayor of the city I one day wanted to live in.

But after the 1996 lecture and our conversation, which was nothing special, I walked him and his entourage to his car. As we said our goodbyes, I took the opportunity to challenge him.

You see, Young is my fraternity brother in Alpha Phi Alpha. He became a member in 1950 at Howard University and I followed in 1989 at NCCU. A challenge is our way of proving that we are a brother, while verifying that the other man is a brother.

When I threw out the challenge, he paused for a moment, then looked at me, smiled, and answered — he reached out his hand, not to shake it in the traditional way, but to share the secret handshake that men in our

Author Ernie Suggs and Ambassador Young admire Young's Alpha Phi Alpha fraternity paddle. Both are members of the oldest Black fraternity in the world, dating back to 1906.

fraternity have closely guarded since 1906.

"My brother," he said as he got in the car.

A year later, I was in Atlanta, writing for the Atlanta Journal-Constitution. Almost since my first day on the AJC, my job has been to cover the city's black community. Atlanta was the "Mecca" of black America, with an unbroken string of black mayors dating back to Maynard Jackson. It was becoming the hub of black culture through fashion and this new form of music called hip-hop.

Most importantly, it was the birthplace of the civil rights movement. And in 1997, all the legends, whom I have called "America's second set of Founders," were living in Atlanta. What a blessing it has been to cover and get to personally know Coretta Scott King, John Lewis, Hosea Williams, Juanita Abernathy, James Orange, C. T. Vivian (whose old Brooks Brothers tie I still wear), and the Reverend Joseph Lowery, who officiated my wedding ceremony.

And, of course, Andrew Young. The thing about him is that he is always around, always accessible. Always willing to share a story, while providing layers upon layers of context.

When last I checked, I had written more than 250 stories in which Young was mentioned. My first, about his walking out of the hospital following a prostate cancer operation. My latest, about his sheer joy of witnessing the Atlanta Braves win the 2021 World Series. In between, I have written about him at his best and his worst. He never complained and simply moved along. Ready to accept my call the next time I needed him.

Throughout my now more than twenty-five years of covering him, I have observed how people address Young, and I see that as a testament to all he has contributed to this world: My Leader. Congressman. Mayor. Ambassador. Reverend. Uncle Andy.

I choose to call him Brother.

My Brother, Andrew Young.

THE MANY LIVES

— OF —

ANDREW YOUNG

I was born by the

river...

EARLY YEARS

DOWNTOWN
NEW ORLEANS
CIRCA 1930s

WHEN ANDY YOUNG WAS GROWING UP IN NEW ORLEANS IN THE 1930S, HIS PROMINENT DENTIST FATHER, ANDREW JACKSON YOUNG SR., TRIED TO TEACH HIM BOXING AS SELF-DEFENSE.

White kids in the neighborhood had started calling Andy and his younger brother, Walter, "niggers" when they walked home from school. Dr. Young would playfully slap-jab his son in the face, a strategy to confuse and frustrate him. On cue, Andy would flail his arms wildly. "Stop that," Dr. Young said. "Don't get mad, get smart. Never lose your head when you get hit."

Dr. Young was talking about boxing, but "don't get mad, get smart" was a mantra that would carry his oldest son out of New Orleans, to the middle of the civil rights movement, to Congress, to the United Nations, to the mayor's office of a major Southern city, to a retirement filled with philanthropy.

Andrew Jackson Young Jr. was born on March 12, 1932, during the Great Depression, just under a year before President Franklin D. Roosevelt was inaugurated for the first of his four terms.

The economic crisis gripping the nation was brutal, but Dr. Young's dental practice and the schoolteacher's income of his wife, Daisy Fuller Young, made the family relatively middle class. Meaning they owned their shotgun house in an inner-city neighborhood shared with Protestants, Catholics, Blacks, whites, Creoles, and even Nazis. Andrew Young would later say that as sober and disciplined as was his world at home, outside the bounds of "school and church and the confines of our little block was the exotic and pulsating city of New Orleans with its riverfront worldliness."

Young Andy became fascinated with the Mississippi River, whose bridges he would often cross when accompanying Dr. Young on trips to provide free dental care to indigent patients in rural Louisiana. This was an early lesson in the importance of helping others.

Andy's grandmother, Louisa Czarnowski Fuller, raised eight of her own children and informally adopted several others. She read the Bible religiously and was known in the community as a woman who would feed anybody who was hungry.

"My life as a middle-class African American was the direct result of my parents' hard work and frugality."

Young also understood the importance of education and the meaning of Black achievement. Even in a segregated school system, he landed at one of New Orleans' best Black elementary schools, which had high expectations for its students and peppered the curriculum with visits from any Black celebrity who visited the city, from Joe Louis to Marian Anderson.

Young attended high school at Gilbert Academy, where he paid $3.50 a month in tuition and began running track and swimming competitively. He was also becoming a member of what the great scholar W. E. B. Du Bois called "The Talented Tenth" —the top 10 percent of Blacks who achieved the greatest success and then were expected to uplift the race.

Andrew Jackson Young Jr. was on his way.

Left: Family photo in New Orleans 1947.
Foreground Left: Andrew Young as a teenager.
Background: New Orleans circa 1940s.
Right: Walter (*brother*) and Andrew Young.

Left: Family neighborhood Andrew was raised in.
Right: Andrew Young as a toddler.

You know, if I could sing, I'd start with Sam Cooke.

"I was born by the river/in a shotgun house..."
in New Orleans, Louisiana.

I was one block off Canal Street, which meant I was right in the middle of the town.

There was an Irish grocery store on one corner. There was an Italian bar on another corner. The headquarters of the Nazi Party was on the third corner, and a Chevrolet dealership was around the fourth corner.

It was a predominantly white neighborhood though there were black families that lived in the neighborhood, but no black children.

I was born into my destiny.

I had to be an ambassador and a negotiator to get to the grocery store and not get beat up. My father was a dentist and my mother started out as a schoolteacher.

New Orleans was a very international city. Well, I guess we were international. My mother was Creole. My father was kind of a combination of black and Indian. My mother's grandfather was Polish and ran a Polish shipping line.

It made for a nice, mixed-up culture. We had access to a variety of cultures which showed up in the cooking, and it showed up in the reading. I never thought of it that way, but I was probably born more of an international citizen.

OF THE MISSISSIPPI RIVER

My father left Straight College and went to Howard University to complete dental school. My mother was teaching then, and teachers weren't allowed to marry, so my parents were engaged for six years before they actually married in 1931. My mother then stopped teaching school and started working as a secretary to an insurance company.

By that time my father was working for Governor Huey Long and the state of Louisiana during the Great Depression. Huey Long hired the doctors and dentists, especially the Black ones, because they were the only ones who didn't mind working for the state.

My father also had a dental trailer. He would drive all over the state with the trailer behind him. He'd pull into various parish courthouses, plug in the water and electricity, and the social workers would line up the children and the elderly, and he fixed their teeth. He stayed until he took care of all of them.

I rode with him sometimes. That gave me a chance to get to know rural Louisiana and especially to become fascinated with the Mississippi River. There were no bridges over the river then, and the river would twist and turn, and to get to the next city you'd have to get on a ferry and go across the Mississippi River.

I was reading Tom Sawyer and Huckleberry Finn and I got enamored with the culture of Louisiana and the Mississippi River.

"I was born into my destiny."

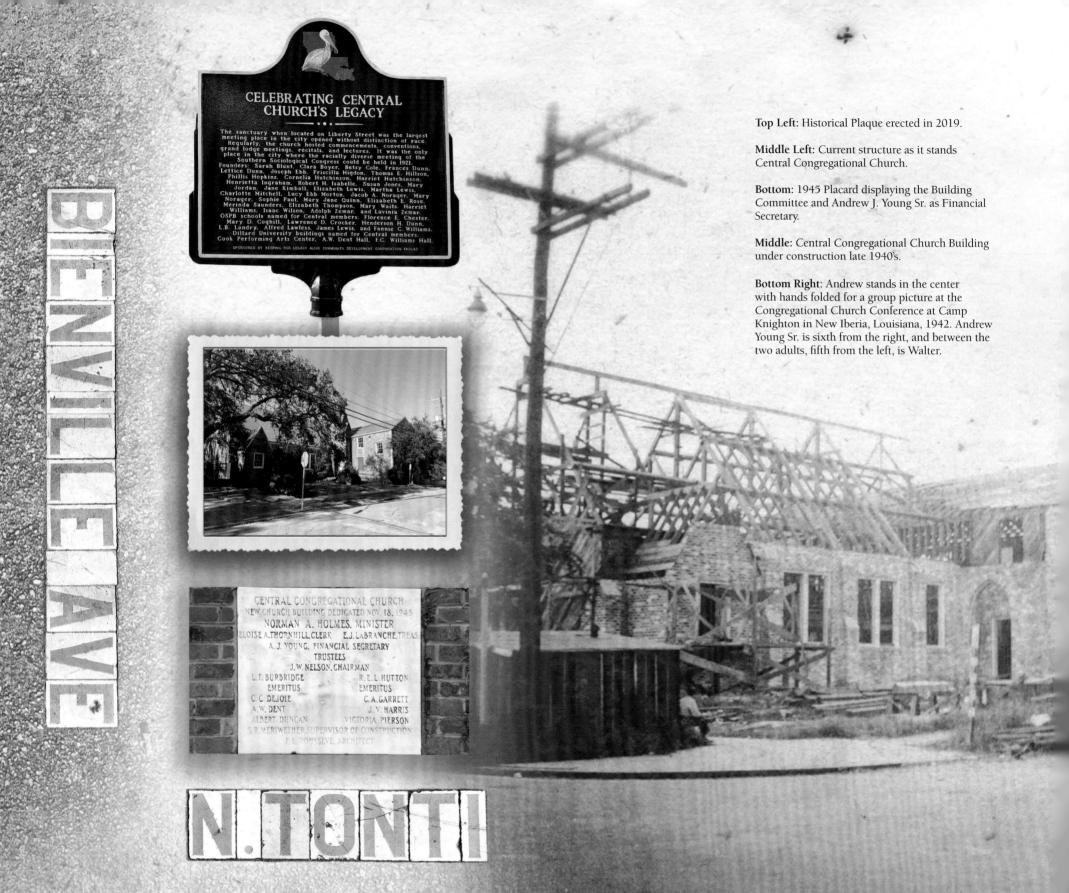

CELEBRATING CENTRAL CHURCH'S LEGACY

The sanctuary when located on Liberty Street was the largest meeting place in the city opened without distinction of race. Regularly, the church hosted commencements, conventions, grand lodge meetings, recitals, and lectures. It was the only place in the city where the racially diverse meeting of the Southern Sociological Congress could be held in 1921. Founders: Sarah Blunt, Clara Boyer, Betsy Cole, Frances Dunn, Lettice Dunn, Joseph Ebb, Priscilla Higdon, Thomas E. Hillson, Phillis Hopkins, Cornelia Hutchinson, Harriet Hutchinson, Henrietta Ingraham, Robert H. Isabelle, Susan Jones, Mary Jordan, Jane Kimball, Elizabeth Lewis, Martha Lewis, Charlotte Mitchell, Lucy Ebb Morton, Jacob A. Norager, Mary Norager, Sophie Paul, Mary Jane Quinn, Elizabeth E. Rose, Merinda Saunders, Elizabeth Thompson, Mary Waits, Harriet Williams, Isaac Wilson, Adolph Zemar, and Lavinia Zemar. OSPB schools named for Central members: Florence E. Chester, Mary D. Coghill, Lawrence D. Crocker, Henderson H. Dunn, L.B. Landry, Alfred Lawless, James Lewis, and Fannie C. Williams. Dillard University buildings named for Central members: Cook Performing Arts Center, A.W. Dent Hall, F.C. Williams Hall.

SPONSORED BY KEEPING OUR LEGACY ALIVE COMMUNITY DEVELOPMENT CORPORATION (KOLA)

CENTRAL CONGREGATIONAL CHURCH
NEW CHURCH BUILDING DEDICATED NOV. 18, 1945
NORMAN A. HOLMES, MINISTER
ELOISE A. THORNHILL, CLERK   E.J. LaBRANCHE, TREAS.
A.J. YOUNG, FINANCIAL SECRETARY
TRUSTEES
J.W. NELSON, CHAIRMAN
L.T. BURBRIDGE   R.E.L. HUTTON
EMERITUS   EMERITUS
C.C. DEJOIE   C.A. GARRETT
A.W. DENT   J.V. HARRIS
ALBERT DUNCAN   VICTORIA PIERSON
S.R. MERIWETHER, SUPERVISOR OF CONSTRUCTION
E.L. ROUSSEVE, ARCHITECT

Top Left: Historical Plaque erected in 2019.

Middle Left: Current structure as it stands Central Congregational Church.

Bottom: 1945 Placard displaying the Building Committee and Andrew J. Young Sr. as Financial Secretary.

Middle: Central Congregational Church Building under construction late 1940's.

Bottom Right: Andrew stands in the center with hands folded for a group picture at the Congregational Church Conference at Camp Knighton in New Iberia, Louisiana, 1942. Andrew Young Sr. is sixth from the right, and between the two adults, fifth from the left, is Walter.

BIENVILLE AVE

N. TONTI

I was grounded in my New Orleans neighborhood, but I went to nursery school at the Central Congregational Church. They taught me to read and write by the time I was three to four years old.

When it came time to go to public schools, they didn't put me in first grade or kindergarten. They put me in third grade. I was six, but most of my classmates were nine to twelve and that put me at a disadvantage. But it also was a challenge. An attempt to meet that challenge got me put out of school in third grade.

I was playing with the biggest, baddest boy in the class. We were playing mumblety-peg with an ice pick in the back of the room. It was a big class of sixty people and they didn't care about us and we didn't care about them. But I had enough common sense to make friends with the biggest, baddest

boy in the class to keep from getting beat up and to keep anybody from taking my lunch money.

I was adjusting pretty well, except that when we got put out, I immediately went across the street to the drugstore and called my parents. My mother stopped what she was doing, came over, and got me back in school. The other little fella — I don't know his last name, but his first name was Lincoln — was twice my size, but he never came back.

"Lincoln said: 'If I ever hear that you dropped out of school, I will kick your ass. I will beat the living shit out of you. Here I am, I haven't been back in school since third grade. And you got a chance to go to high school and college."

Years later, I went to Howard University and I was on the swimming team.

Back home in the summers, I worked at the local swimming pool and one day this fellow fell into the deep water and the other lifeguard and I pulled him out. It was Lincoln. He reminded me that we had been put out of the third grade. I said, 'Where have you been?' And he said, 'I've been in and out of every reform school and jail in the state of Louisiana.'

He said, "Wait, what are you doing?" I said, "Well, I'm in college at Howard University, but I don't want to be there. My daddy wants me to be a dentist, but I know I'm not going to be a dentist. And I'm thinking of dropping out."

Lincoln said: "If I ever hear that you dropped out of school, I will kick your ass. I will beat the living shit out of you. Here I am, I haven't been back in school since third grade. And you got a chance to go to high school and college."

The truth of it is that I had been all over the country. I went to Dillard University for one year. I got a ride out to California and went to the University of Southern California for a summer. Some friends of mine were going into Boston and I hitched a ride with them and took a summer at Boston University . . . and I was about to graduate or drop out from Howard University.

And Lincoln said: "I better not hear that you didn't graduate. I'm as smart as you, you know that, don't you? If I had the chances you had, I never would have wasted them the way you wasted them."

You put all that together, and that's one hell of a childhood.

Top Left: College Photo circa 1940s.
Bottom Left: Young's Home during his teen years.

Bottom 2nd from Left: Valena C. Jones Elementary School, New Orleans, circa 1930's.

Middle Bottom: Gilbert Academy High School.

Bottom Right: Andrew Young's 1950 Lifeguard Card.

THE AMERICAN NATIONAL RED CROSS

ANDREW JACKSON YOUNG, INSTRUCTOR IS AUTHORIZED TO CONDUCT Swimming, Life Saving, and Water Safety Courses FOR THE

NEW ORLEANS, LOUISIANA CHAPTER

FOR THE PERIOD JAN. 1, 1950 to DEC. 31, 1950

CHAPTER REPRESENTATIVE

AREA DIRECTOR
FIRST AID, WATER SAFETY AND ACCIDENT PREVENTION

"He grew up in Franklin, Louisiana. He was educated, but I don't know where or how. He had somewhere between $4 and $5 million in the bank in, you know, 1910."

My Grandfather

FRANK SMITH YOUNG

My daddy also played baseball, up in the Catskills to get money to go through school.
The country clubs competed against each other.

And if you were hitting and fielding well, you got the good tables and you got good tips. That's the way he paid his way through dental school. Not because his father didn't have any money, but his father wouldn't pay his way. That's the mystery of my life. I don't know how my grandfather got to be my grandfather. I mean, I don't know. He grew up in Franklin, Louisiana. He was educated, but I don't know where or how. He had somewhere between $4 and $5 million in the bank in, you know, 1910.

But he wouldn't pay my dad's tuition with it. He had a burial society, Prince Hall Masons, the Odd Fellows. I mean, there were all kinds of Masonic lodges that he seemed to be the treasurer of. So, while the family lived well and all of my parents got an education, it was not a luxurious life. He made my father work his way through dental school. Actually, this is 2021. My father graduated from Howard University's dental school in 1921. So, this is 100 years out of dental school

this year. Any way you look at that, this was during the post-Reconstruction, during the Ku Klux Klan and all of the racism in the South. And yet my relatives adjusted to it, or they handled it and they carved a place for themselves.

I remember one of the stories they told about my grandfather was that they'd just built the charity hospital in New Orleans and they didn't have any black nurses. And so, everybody ran to my grandfather and said, 'you got to go see the governor.' We got to have black nurses in charity hospital. Huey Long promised him that he would have black nurses in the hospital Monday morning. And he came back and told the other black leaders that they said, oh, no, he's pulling your leg. Ain't no way he can get them by Monday morning.

On Monday morning Huey Long gets up before the state legislature and starts on this long tirade about the Southern white woman and that the Southern white woman is the fairest flower on God's earth. And he talked about the blue eyes and the blonde hair and the sparkling pearl, radiant skin. And he went on for a half hour about the beauty of the white woman.

And then he said, but it grieves me to my death that God's fairest flower on earth has to take care of them big, black, burly bucks. We got to get some nurses in the hospital to take care of their own men. And they jumped up and they shouted, and they appropriated the money and they got black nurses in the hospital. That's the Louisiana south. Growing up in that kind of environment really suited me when I got to the United nations. I mean that when I had to go see Ian Smith in Zimbabwe or Rhodesia or P.W. Botha in South Africa, or any of the really ruthless and brutal racists that were governing the apartheid states, I felt like I knew them. And so, my childhood has led to my adulthood and it was very good preparation.

Left: Frank Smith Young, *Portrait.*

Bottom: Andrew Young standing in front of his grandfather's home in Franklin, Louisiana.

My Grandmother:

LOUISA CZARNOWSKI FULLER

On my mother's side of the family, they were Creole.

They were very fair-skinned with straight hair. My grandmother had these long tresses that she would brush every day. She lost her sight when she was around eighty. I was about nine or ten, and it became my job to read the newspaper and the Bible to her every day as soon as I came home from school. What I got in school was one form of education. But what I got at home from my grandmother was another kind of, really very religious education. She had lost her sight and would fuss with God. So, when I'm reading the Bible, she would give it her interpretation, but she wasn't just talking to me, she was talking to God. She would say things like, 'Lord, I raised eleven children and only five are mine. I don't know how I got to be taking care of everybody else's children, but I did my duty. I have lived as good a life as I can, and I'm ready to come home and get my reward.'

She prayed every day for God to take her home. She didn't want to be blind, and she didn't want to be a burden on the family. That made me feel very, very comfortable with death. Death was not something you fear. Death was something you look forward to. Interestingly, when I met Martin Luther King, I learned he had the same kind of relationship with his grandmother.

So death was not something that he feared. It was inevitable. He'd say death is the ultimate democracy. I don't care how rich you are, how black you are, how white you are, whatever you are, you're going to die, and there's no escaping death. And you have nothing to say about when you die or how you die. The only thing you have any control over is what is it you give your life for. Between the two of them, I grew up feeling very comfortable in this spiritual universe.

My father, my mother, all were very religious, and we went to church every Sunday. Went to Sunday school. Went to Bible study on Wednesday night. We were basically a church family. That was sort of who I am and how I got to be that way. And all I think of it is that I have lived a blessed life by no virtue of my own.

That's the way I was placed in this universe. But one thing my grandmother always said, 'Now, Son, you've been blessed. And to those to whom much has been given, of them is much required. He didn't say 'suggested.' Because of your blessings, you have to pass on those blessings to others. You can't have much better lessons than that.

> "She lost her sight when she was around eighty years old. I was about nine or ten and it became my job to read the newspaper and the Bible to her every day."

Left: Louisa Czarnowski Fuller, circa 1940's,
Left Middle: Larger portrait when she was 80.
Bottom Left: Andrew on a pony in 1933.
Bottom Right: Andrew and Walter in the alley between their home as their grandmother pushes them.

"Don't get mad,
get smart."

I got my diplomatic lessons and my life lessons, it seems from my father.

My aunt lived two doors behind the Nazi Party. So, I had to go by there two- three times a week. I was four years old and my father, walking by, said, 'these are white supremacists and white supremacy is a sickness. You know that God made of one blood, all the nations of the earth. But they don't want to admit that, but that is not your problem. That is their problem. You don't need to try to convert them. Neither do you need to be angry with them.'

He took me to the MovieTone News to see Jesse Owens in the 1936 Olympics. And I am four years old. When Jesse Owens won the 100-meter dash, Hitler was supposed to present him with his Olympic medallion. He refused to do this and stormed out of the stadium, which was an insult.

But my father said, 'that was not Jesse's problem. That was Hitler's problem.' And Jesse focused on his business and he just went on and won three more gold medals and broke a couple of world records.

So, he said, 'You don't get mad in a confrontation like this.' And his motto was, 'Don't get mad, get smart.'

When you have a conflict, you decide in your mind what the situation is, and it doesn't matter what they call you. It doesn't matter what they say about you. You know that this is their sickness and not yours. And the worst thing you can do is get angry at some sick person.

He was a dentist and he said, you know, I know that these white people, if they'd come to me two weeks ago, I might've saved their teeth, but they'll wait until it's abscessed and call me in the middle of the night and want me to stop the pain. And he said, 'I do because my job is being a healer. It doesn't help me or them to get mad.'

So that was the very practical way that he dealt with my problems in the neighborhood. Now, my mother, my grandmother and my younger brother all lived in that house. It was also a house where my father had his dental office. It meant that there were people coming in and out of there all the time. And I can remember running in the office and just flying through the office, back to my room.

My father stopped what he was doing. And he came back, and he got me, and he brought me by my hand, and he took me to, and he said, now introduce yourself to each one of these patients. He said, these are the people who are going to pay your tuition to college, and you can't run by and ignore and not speak to them. They're interested in you; they're investing in you. So, the least you can do is show your appreciation for them. And so that's where I got my mandate to respect everybody.

Anytime I ran through his office, I had to stop, shake hands, and speak to every one of his patients. That was all my life, but that's what made me sensitive to people. And he said, they want to get to know you and you need to get to know them. You can learn a lot from other people. Louis Armstrong was one of his patients. Fats Pichon was a big, fat piano player. And we had a little piano in the office. Whenever he came, he played the piano and sang the blues. It was quite a lively office. Most of his patients were black, but not all. Most of his dental supply people were white. It was an interracial environment. Most of the dental suppliers happened to be Jewish and with the Nazi Party right on the corner, there was always conversation about what was going on in Germany.

That was just a part of my life. It meant that I was born into the Arab-Israeli situation that was just before, Ralph Bunche and Count Bernadette negotiated the peace that gave Israel its identity and its nationality.

My Mother:
DAISY FULLER YOUNG

February 7, 1969

Dear Mother + Daddy,

It will soon be your anniversary. You admit to 38 years together, and yet I can't help but believe that spiritually you have been together closer to 45 years. So far as I am concerned, they have been wonderful years. You have given us an ideal for marriage that is hard to follow. I was fortunate to find a wife with similar family precident, so it has been relatively easy for us to follow in your loving example, but it takes two to make a family and that both have to be willing to work and suffer to grow "together as one".

You have done your task well. I don't think that two children could want for any more love, inspiration, care or comfort than Walt + I received. We were and are wonderfully blessed to have you as parents.

If we have erred in any respect, it was due more to the special tensions and pressures of life itself in this second half of this twentieth century and not in any way to deficiencies in our up-bringing.

Andrew J. Young

Top Right: Walter and Andrew pose with their mother 1930's.

Left: SCLC Letter to Andrew's parents 1969.

Middle: Daisy Fuller Young.

Middle Bottom: Walter and Andrew during Mardi Gras, in New Orleans.

Top Right: Postcard from Paris to his Andrew's parents.

Right: Daisy Fuller Young (*mother*).

My Mother

MY MOTHER, Daisy Fuller Young, was the youngest of eight children and a pure product of a New Orleans family of classic Creole complexity. She barely knew her father, but she could trace her family back to the 1840s. A ship captain named Brown bought and freed her great-grandmother to enter into a relationship with her that produced several children.

All of the children could pass for white except my grandmother, Louisa. Then my mother and all of her siblings were fair-skinned, some to the point where they avoided declaring themselves "colored," so they could get better jobs and access.

Even my mother's sisters warned her against marrying my father because he was a dentist who wouldn't be able to properly support her. As a light-skinned Creole, she would have more options.

My parents met at Straight College, which was one of the first places in the Deep South that blacks could get a college education. My father had already graduated, but he returned to campus for a visit and met my mother, who was getting her teacher's certificate.

They married in 1931 and I was born in 1932. My father was the head of our household, but my mother ran his life. My mother managed his dental office and made sure it was successful. She kept the accounts and made sure that patients' bills were paid on time.

My mother was very protective, and despite the fact that she was a staunch Congregationalist, when my brother Walter and I first went off to elementary school, she would go to the Catholic church every day to say novenas for our welfare. When I was old enough to run errands for her downtown, she always insisted that I wear a shirt and tie as a symbol of our middle-class status—but she also feared that I would be accused of stealing.

Even when I was at Howard, she came up with a scheme to continue washing my clothes. One of our New Orleans neighbors worked for the Southern Railroad. Every week, I would meet him at the train station in Washington and hand him a bag of dirty clothes, which he would deliver to my mother. She would wash them, and he would bring them back to me in Washington.

COLLEGE

Veritas et Utilitas

ANDREW YOUNG'S EDUCATION WAS ALWAYS A GIVEN. HIS MOTHER, DAISY FULLER YOUNG, A FORMER TEACHER, HAD GRADUATED FROM STRAIGHT COLLEGE. ANDREW YOUNG SR. ALSO ATTENDED STRAIGHT, BEFORE MOVING TO WASHINGTON, D.C., TO ATTEND DENTAL SCHOOL AT THE PRESTIGIOUS HOWARD UNIVERSITY, GRADUATING IN 1921.

Young graduated from Gilbert Academy in 1947. Because he was only fifteen, his parents wanted to keep him close by. He enrolled as a freshman at Dillard University, a historically Black college that was formed in 1934 during the Great Depression after a merger between New Orleans University and the financially struggling Straight College.

By his sophomore year, his parents let him transfer to Howard University, then the largest Black college in America. He was among the youngest students on campus and struggled socially, among the older women, and academically, where he was in classrooms with older students, many of whom were World War II veterans. Young still made both the swimming and track teams, and, despite finding Howard sometimes "imbued with haughtiness," slowly found his social niche. He watched how older African students would study and take classes so seriously. He pledged Alpha Phi Alpha fraternity, where an older classmate, David Dinkins, the future first Black mayor of New York City, took him under his wing and gave protection.

He even got a girlfriend, the only child of a local physician. She was as demanding as she was beautiful. A biology major, Young graduated from Howard in 1951, with expectations of going to dental school to follow his father's path.

Young admitted that he graduated more "thank you Lordy" than magna cum laude and was one D away from not graduating at all. But he also acknowledged that while he may have been a lackadaisical Howard student, he matured a lot and "learned how to embrace the strengths of the Black middle class."

Yet, as his parents drove him from Washington back to New Orleans after graduation, he sat in the backseat of their Oldsmobile and wondered, "What will be required?"

HOWARD UNIVERSITY

"I had a feeling that more was expected of me."

Bottom: Andrew pledged Alpha Phi Alpha at Howard University in 1950. In the bottom photo, he is sixth from the right. Andrew's dean of pledges was future New York City Mayor David Dinkins (*first on the left*).

My father wanted me to be a dentist
and a baseball player.

My father wanted me to be a dentist and a baseball player. He loved dentistry and he was a very good baseball player. He would get out in the street in front of the house and throw the ball to me. We'd play pitch and catch. He'd throw it on the ground, and he'd throw it in the air. He had me running down the street trying to catch the ball over my shoulder, like Willie Mays. He really wanted me to be a good athlete and a good student. I was so-so at both, mainly because there was no place to play baseball in New Orleans.

He believed in dentistry because he believed in security. And his only reason was if you're a dentist, you'd make $10,000 a year and you can own a home and you can send your children to college and you can be a responsible father. That was basically his goal—to make sure I had enough education to take care of a family.

I had a feeling that more was expected of me than that. I didn't know what and I didn't care. I liked science so I took botany at the University of Southern California. I took a whole year of physics in six weeks at Boston University. I had to go to summer school because I didn't do a lot of studying at Howard.

At Howard I was trying to be a swimmer and a member of the track team. Going to college in 1947 at age fifteen with all of the veterans coming back from the military, I had a hard time keeping up.

Dave Dinkins, who later became mayor of New York City, sorta took me in. We were in the same fraternity, but he was like twenty-two and I was fifteen, and he'd been in the Marine Corps.

The other people who looked out for me in college were the foreign students. One of my friends was a Nigerian who had a double major in chemistry and physics and a double minor in math and psychology. He finished his undergraduate program in two years.

He studied all the time. He felt that you didn't need more than four hours of sleep at night. When he was getting up to study in the middle of the night, he would say to me, "You are a bright boy. If you ever get civilized, you could be somebody." He ended up going to McGill medical school and finishing at the top of his class in neurosurgery. Went back to Nigeria and was the minister of public health. He performed neurosurgery, taught neurosurgery at the medical school, and was the dean of the medical school. He had four jobs. He worked nearly twenty hours a day. He did not live long though. I don't think he lived to be sixty. When I started going to Nigeria, I looked for him and I saw they had named streets and buildings at the medical school for him, but he had worked himself to death.

I liked my studies, but I didn't take them that seriously. I had no trouble passing courses, but A's and B's were for foreign students and veterans. I was trying to become a man, and I can't think of a better place to have come into my manhood than Howard University. There were ten thousand students. There was a law school, an engineering school, a medical school and a dental school.

But my interests were sports and girls. I was better at sports than I was at girls. I was short and I was three years younger than even the girls in my freshman class. Most of them were eighteen or nineteen. I was fifteen.

I don't know what Howard University did for me, but there was all the difference in the world between the University of Southern California and Howard University. Nobody spoke to me for almost an entire summer at the University of Southern California. I did make friends at Boston University a few years later, but I made friends because a group of girls came from Howard to Boston University for summer school. And I had a network of friends.

I got involved in the sports life and the fraternity life. Both gave me a sense of confidence and security. The hazing and the bullying of young fraternity members was always challenging, but I wouldn't pay them any attention.

I would not let them get the best of me. For instance, they said, if you're going to join Alpha Phi Alpha, you gotta drink this whole half pint of bourbon to show that you're a man. I said, no, I don't. And he said, well, you gonna drink it or I'm gonna pour it on you. I said, no, you're not. Dave Dinkins came to my rescue. He said, either you're going to drink this, or you're gonna run ten miles around the reservoir. I didn't even answer, I just took off and started running. It was a wonderful time.

Left: Andrew (third from the right) on line for the Beta Chapter of Alpha Phi Alpha at Howard University in 1950.

Middle Left: Andrew boarding the train.

Left Bottom: Howard dancers practicing their routine.

Right: Daisy Fuller Young.

Right: Andrew running track 1950.

"At Howard I was trying to be a swimmer and a member of the track team and. Really, going to college at fifteen with all of the veterans coming back from the military in 1947, I had a hard time keeping up."

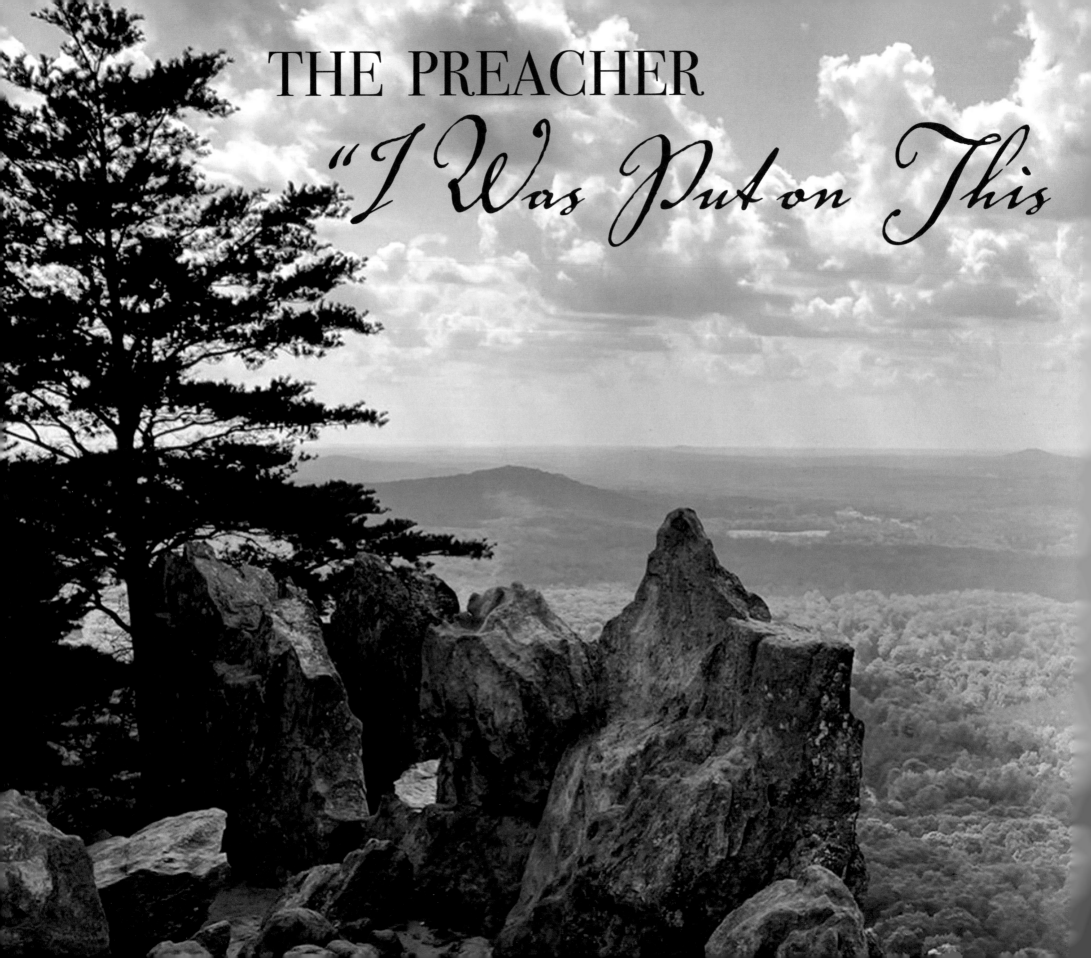

THE PREACHER
"I Was Put on This

Earth for Some Purpose."

ON A TRIP THROUGH THE SOUTH IN JUNE 1951, THE YOUNG FAMILY MADE A STOP IN KINGS MOUNTAIN, NORTH CAROLINA, WHERE THE CONVENTION OF THE SOUTH OF THE CONGREGATIONAL CHURCH WAS HOLDING ITS SUMMER CONFERENCE.

Young had just graduated from Howard University and decided not to go to dental school or do like other recent college graduates in those days and get married. Trying out to run in the Olympics was on his mind but momentarily he was lost. While his parents were at the Convention, Young put on his shorts and sneakers to run up Kings Mountain. He ran and ran. Thinking about New Orleans and Howard. Thinking about how he was raised and the church. Thinking about the Olympics. Faster and faster. He reached the top of the mountain and collapsed. When he opened his eyes, he saw the beauty of the vista in front of him. Just like that, he saw the order of the universe, thinking that "surely there is a God, the creator of heaven and earth. Suddenly, from the top of Kings Mountain my whole life began anew." An awakening occurred.

After arriving back in New Orleans, Young caught a ride to Texas with the Reverend Nicholas Hood, the pastor of Central Church in New Orleans. Hood was to lead a retreat in Texas. It was there that Young finally decided that he was not going to dental school but would attend seminary to become a minister.

He traveled to Hartford, Connecticut. To work as an organizer for United Christian Youth Action. He took advantage of his living situation at Hartford Theological Seminary and enrolled in two classes. He asked the dean if he could enroll full-time and was admitted, despite his poor

grades at Howard. To pay for his education, Young took on three jobs. And unlike at Howard, he excelled in his classes. In the summer of 1952, although he had planned on being on the Olympic team, he was asked to travel to tiny Marion, Alabama, to be a summer assistant at a church. He was reluctant to go, but it would be in Marion where he met his first wife, Jean Childs, whom he would marry in 1954.

After graduating with a Bachelor of Divinity degree from Hartford Theological Seminary in 1955, Young became ordained in the United Church of Christ. He, Jean, and their newborn daughter Andrea, soon moved to Thomasville, Georgia, to take the pastorate of Bethany Congregational Church. Meanwhile, Young had started to read the works of Mahatma Gandhi and related to the concept of nonviolence as a tactic for social change.

After two years in Georgia, Young was recruited to move to New York City and work as an associate director in the youth department of the National Council of Churches. He was conflicted over the move. He had just gotten to Thomasville and was making a name for himself as the town's young Black preacher. He finally agreed to take the New York job, under one condition from Jean—that they would return to the South within "four to five" years. That was 1957.

33 [a] Sell that ye have, and give alms; [c] provide yourselves bags which wax not old, a treasure in the heavens that faileth not, where no thief approacheth, neither moth corrupteth.

34 For where your treasure is, there will your heart be also.

35 [e] Let your loins be girded about, and [f] *your* lights burning;

36 And ye yourselves like unto men that wait for their lord, when ...

A.D. 33.
[a] Mat. 19. 21.
Acts 2. 45.
& 4. 34.
[b] Num. 15. 30.
Deut. 25. 2.
John 9. 41.
& 15. 22.
Acts 17. 30.
James 4. 17.
[c] Mat. 6. 20.
ch. 16. 9.
1 Tim. 6. 19.
[d] Lev. 5. 17.
1 Tim. 1. 13.
[e] Eph. 6. 14.
1 Pet. 1. 13.
[f] Mat. 25. 1, &c.
[g] ver. 51.

47 And [b] that servant, which knew his lord's will, and prepared not *himself*, neither did according to his will, shall be beaten with many stripes.

48 [d] But he that knew not, and did commit things worthy of stripes, shall be beaten with few *stripes.* For unto whomsoever much is given, of him shall be much required: and to whom men have committed much, of him they will ask the more.

49 ¶ [g] I am come to send fire on ...th; and what will I, if it be kindled?

... [h] I have a baptism to be

---

56   *A Testament of Devotion*

awful immediacy. There is an indelicacy in too-ready speech. Paul felt it unlawful to speak of the things of the third heaven. But there is also a false reticence, as if these things were one's own work and one's own possession, about which we should modestly keep quiet, whereas they are wholly God's amazing work and we are nothing, mere passive receivers. "The lion hath roared, who can but tremble? The voice of Jehovah hath spoken, who can but prophesy?" (Amos 3:8).

Some men come into holy obedience through the gateway of profound mystical experience.

It is an overwhelming experience to fall into the hands of the living God, to be invaded to the depths of one's being by His presence, to be, without warning, wholly uprooted from all earth-born securities and assurances, and to be blown by a tempest of unbelievable power which leaves one's old proud self utterly, utterly defenseless, until one cries, "All Thy waves and thy billows are gone over me" (Ps. 42:7). Then is the soul swept into a Loving Center of ineffable sweetness, where calm and unspeakable peace and ravishing joy steal over one. And one knows now why Pascal wrote, in the center of his greatest moment, the single word, "Fire." There stands the world of struggling, sinful, earth-blinded men and nations, of plants and animals and wheeling stars of heaven, all new, all lapped in the tender, persuading

Mysticism

Holy Obedience   57

Love at the Center. There stand the saints of the ages, their hearts open to view, and lo, their hearts are our heart and their hearts are the heart of the Eternal One. In awful solemnity the Holy One is over all and in all, exquisitely loving, infinitely patient, tenderly smiling. Marks of glory are upon all things, and the marks are cruciform and blood-stained. And one sighs, like the convinced Thomas of old, "My Lord and my God" (John 20:28). Dare one lift one's eyes and look? Nay, whither *can* one look and not see Him? For field and stream and teeming streets are full of Him. Yet as Moses knew, no man can look on God and live—live as his old self. Death comes, blessed death, death of one's alienating will. And one knows what Paul meant when he wrote, "The life which I now live in the flesh I live by the faith of the Son of God" (Gal. 2:20).

One emerges from such soul-shaking, Love-invaded times into more normal states of consciousness. But one knows ever after that the Eternal Lover of the world, the Hound of Heaven, is utterly, utterly real, and that life must henceforth be forever determined by that Real. Like Saint Augustine one asks not for greater certainty of God but only for more steadfastness in Him. There, beyond, in Him is the true Center, and we are reduced, as it were, to nothing, for He is all.

Is religion subjective? Nay, its soul is in objectivity,

January, 1952

Sun 6 — Providence M.Y.F.

Mon 7 Universal Wk. Prayer Westerly - 7:30 Pawcatuck Cong. Ch.

Tues 8 Woonsocket 7:00 Universalist Church

Wed 9 W. Warwick - 7:30 Riverpoint Cong. Pawtucket Minis 12 noon Smithfield Cong.

Thurs 10 — Exam

Fri 11 Pascoag 7:30 Comm. Bapt. Cranston 7:30 Phill. Mem

When I got close to graduation, I really wasn't sure I was going to graduate. I mean, I wasn't interested enough to even check my curriculum to see what courses I'd taken, what my grades were. I was surprised when they had my name on the matriculation list.

But I didn't want my parents to come up. Because all through school, my parents were always looking to see their friends' children shine, and I didn't shine.

But I really got an education, and I had a wonderful time. It was the diversity, because Howard was predominantly black, but it wasn't all black. It was African, it was Middle Eastern. It was Caribbean. A few Asians. I got to understand the world, not from reading books. The books I read were biology books and chemistry books. I really took no philosophy. The only course I took in sociology I got a D in because my professor, who had two doctorates from the Sorbonne and the University of Chicago, was trying to tell me about juvenile delinquency and what the theories were.

And I just said, Dr. K, I'm sorry. It's not that way. You read about it in books, I've been living with delinquents all my life. In my high school class, only a fourth of us went to college and a fourth of us went to the military. The other half went to jail and it wasn't because they were delinquent. It was because they were poor and black. I said all of these books that are talking about the shape of the skull and all of that crap, none of that makes sense. Trust me, I know more hoodlums than any of these guys who wrote these books. Because I would stand up to the professors and argue with them, I didn't get such good grades. I insisted on being independent of everybody.

The track coach didn't want to give me track shoes or a uniform because I was small. I borrowed some shoes from my brother and got in a race and beat everybody. And the coach still didn't want to give me any, so I had to keep my brother's shoes. Part of it was the easy, playful, irresponsible way that I carried myself. I wasn't doing what they wanted me to do, but I was enjoying myself and I was learning, and I was developing.

My swimming coach, I am not even sure he could swim, because he never gave me any pointers. I'd go to the library and check out a book on swimming and coach myself. But I had a wonderful time. I met a wonderful young lady, who quit me when I said I was going into the ministry.

I was supposed to go to New York to train with the Pioneer Track Club for the 1952 Olympics. But my conference superintendent called and said he needed me to go to Alabama. My young lady said, I'm sorry, I am not going south of the Potomac. Her father was one of the wealthiest physicians in town and she was probably the only girl in the city who had her own car. That put an end to a wonderful university life.

When I graduated from Howard, we were driving back to New Orleans and there were no hotels, so we stopped and stayed at a church conference in King's Mountain, North Carolina. I was still interested in running so I went out running while my mother and father were at the church conference. When you're running in the hills around North Carolina, nothing is flat. Everything is either slightly down or slightly up. And I had been running for a couple of miles and I was running down hill and I was running too fast. I was already out of breath and I get to this mountain trail going up to the top of King's Mountain. And I decided I'm going to push right onto the top of the mountain. Well, I wouldn't stop. I kept running. And when I got to the top of the mountain, I really blacked out and couldn't breathe.

I don't know what happened to me, but when I came to and opened my eyes, everything seemed different. You take the sky for granted, but all of a sudden the sky was radiant. You look at a corn field and see this gold and yellow. You look at the forest and the trees and the cows, everything just seemed to radiate life and meaning. It just suddenly hit me that if everything I see has a purpose then whoever made that made everything with a purpose.

If the trees and the cows and the corn and the sky have a purpose, there's gotta be a purpose for me. I didn't know what it was, and I didn't care, but there was a certainty that I was put on this earth for some purpose. My life just changed in that moment of awakening. And I ran back down the hill and didn't get tired.

"(Rev. Hood) said, 'look, I'm from the North and I don't know my way around the South and how to act. Why don't you drive with me?' I said, 'sure.'"

THE TRIP

It was such a sense of confidence and purpose and I didn't know about what. All I have to do is do the best that I can one day at a time, and everything's going to be all right.

Well, that's sorta what happened. I go home and I have a new preacher and he's just graduated from Yale Divinity School. And he's from Terre Haute, Indiana. He's going out in Texas to do Bible study at an interracial conference—there weren't many back in 1951. And he said, look, I'm from the North and I don't know my way around the South and how to act. Why don't you drive with me? I said, sure. He and I were the only two black people there with all of these white kids from the colleges and universities around. There was a big religious movement at the University of Texas then. Most of the kids were part of that and they were all dedicated. They wanted to go someplace as a missionary. I started waking up in the morning and going to the Bible studies, and the Bible now made sense in a way that it didn't before.

My preacher would talk for about ten or fifteen minutes, and we would then scatter and everybody would find a place alone overlooking this lake. And you had a half hour of meditation. Well, I'd never done that before, and it was awakening a new part of my life. All of a sudden, I was beginning to perceive meanings in the scriptures that he was giving. When we got ready to leave, they asked for volunteers to work with the church youth movement, and they particularly put the arm on me because they said, look, we wanted this to be an interracial program, and you're the only Negro to show up.

One of the things I felt when I came down from the mountain was there's something that I can do that nobody else can do. So I volunteered for six months. That ended up with me going to Connecticut to work with the Council of Churches. They didn't have a place for me to live. So, they called the Hartford Theological Seminary and asked if they had an extra room. I really liked that. There were a lot of guys coming back from the military So there was nothing pious about this place. The first guy that I saw looked like a big hillbilly and his

greeting was, "What's a fine young man like you doing at a place like this? Are you running from some woman or you're trying to stay out of the Army?" I wasn't prepared to be greeted like that.

I said, well, probably a little of both. I was comfortable on that campus. I decided since most of my work was after three o'clock that I'd go to the Dean's office and ask if I could sit in on a course on the Old Testament and on the New Testament, because I didn't know enough about the Bible. He added a third course, philosophy of religion, and gave me a scholarship through the Rockefeller brothers fund for Negro ministry. They had the scholarship in the books for years and nobody ever asked for it.

I worked in the Connecticut Council of Churches, and I didn't think of myself as a preacher. We had a conference with three thousand young people in the auditorium in Hartford. I worked out a presentation of slides to explain what this was all about. I'm on the stage and I do the narration for the first slide and nothing happens. I go on to the second slide and nothing happens. By the third slide, I realize I'm making a fool of myself. So I made a half-hour speech. Everybody thought it was wonderful. I hadn't known what I was going to say, but I thought of the passage, "When the Lord delivers you up, the Lord who made your mouth can put words in it."

General Brotherhood Board
Church of the Brethren
INCORPORATED
22 SOUTH STATE STREET
ELGIN, ILLINOIS

6616

OFFICIAL RECEIPT

Fiscal agent of the Church of the Brethren   DATE Apr. 6, 1953

AMOUNT $ 200.00

WE GRATEFULLY ACKNOWLEDGE RECEIPT OF THE ABOVE SUM FROM:

Andrew J. Young
Hartford Seminary Foundation
55 Elizabeth St.
Hartford 5, Conn.

FOR: work camp deposit

4

CHURCH OF THE BRETHREN

General Brotherhood Board

Norman J. Baugher • General Secretary

BRETHREN SERVICE COMMISSION
W. Harold Row, Executive Secretary
22 South State Street, Elgin, Illinois, Phone 5010

March 18, 1953

TO WHOM IT MAY CONCERN:

Andrew J. Young, 55 Elizabeth Street, Hartford 5, Connecticut, has been appointed as a foreign work camper by the Brethren Service Commission, which is the relief agency of the Church of the Brethren with headquarters at 22 South State Street, Elgin, Illinois.

The Church of the Brethren has been doing relief and rehabilitation work in Europe for a number of years, and the appointment of Mr. Young is a part of our normal summer work camp program.

The Church of the Brethren is a member of the American Council of Voluntary Agencies for Foreign Service of 20 West 40th Street, New York, N. Y. and is registered with the President's Advisory Committee on Voluntary Foreign Aid. Our Commission is also cooperating with the Department of Church World Service, of the National Council of the Churches of Christ in the United States of America.

It is our desire to send Mr. Young for a period of three months. He desires to serve the Church and we are sure he will render valuable service to the people with whom he will be working.

Whatever assistance rendered by your office will be appreciated by this Commission.

Sincerely yours,

W. Harold Row

W. Harold Row
Executive Secretary

Middle Right: Through the church Work camp, digging for a foundation for a bombed school in Austria

It evidently made sense. When I was finished with that, I had signed up to go to New York, to run with the Pioneer Track Club. I had a job at a settlement house in Harlem. I got a call from my conference superintendent. I didn't know that my mother had been calling him saying, "Can you help me get Andrew back down South?" And a lady in Marion, Alabama, had said, "We have a church here, and you have not been able to supply us with a minister for the last three summers. If we don't have something going on, we're probably going to lose this church." So, I got a call from the conference superintendent and he said, "I need you to come to Alabama."

I said, "I'm sorry, but I'm going to New York. You know, I've already signed up. I got a job and a place to stay." He said, "Well, if you don't go to New York, somebody will go. Everybody wants to go to New York. You also know that if you are not in this Olympics, the Olympics will go on without you. But there's a little church down in Alabama that if you don't go, we'll lose it. It'll close down for good."

I was trapped by my own philosophy. I agree, I have to go to Alabama. And I go through Washington. My girlfriend quits me. I'm driving, you know, down through the mountains, crying all the way to Atlanta. When I got to Atlanta, I'll never forget, I saw a rat crossing Ponce de Leon and I slowed down for the rat because rats had more rights than black folk in Georgia.

"When I got to Atlanta, I'll never forget, I saw a rat crossing Ponce de Leon and I slowed down for the rat because rats had more rights than black folk in Georgia."

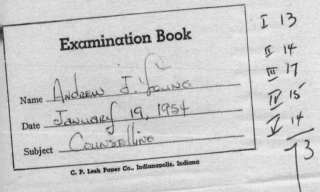

Examination Book

Name Andrew J. Young

Date January 19, 1954

Subject Counselling

C. P. Lesh Paper Co., Indianapolis, Indiana

I 13
II 14
III 17
IV 15
V 14
73

---

1. ——— Introduction
   Difficulty of Preaching...

2. ——— Parable — last mi...
   — Explanation — Nec...
   Middle...

   ——— Illustrations of Doc...
   — Children + Anarchy...
   — Moral laxity in Bus...
   — Failure of Marriage...
   — Actu Howard
   — Materialism
   — Frustration + Anxie...
   Hopeless ? , Yes

3. ——— two streams of...
   — ———
   — Achievement & Fai...
   — Negro unique
   — denial of Heritage...
   — Spiritual las...

---

2 good practical yet imaginative sermons in outline. You have real preaching potential. But you need more finish + thoroughness! You should begin now to write your sermons out in full — for your future power as a preacher

—— I think you have hit on the main p...
when our efforts fail — Apoc. has little if a...
emphasis on human effort — the Christian...
still remains. A.G...

REVELATION 21:1 - 22:5

I. Introduction:
1. Revelation is typical of the ty... of the period just before + a...
2. Date and authorship are dificult... was written by John the aposte... much later.
3. Specific Introduction to this p...
   - deals with perfection of the...
   - the vision is portrayed dra...
   - there is also a symbolism of...
   - the material perfection is... spiritual perfection in the...
   - the metaphors of the Pride... of the loyal. These were for...
   - the marriage is the reconc...
   - there is a combination of... blessedness of the Church...
   - After conclusion of prophecy, -

II Analysis:
1. The passage may be dealt... Christian interpretation of y... an act of God.
2. The Prophecy of the New...
3. The Immanence of Kingdom...

Course grade B—

you missed a number of class sessions and reading reports — otherwise you made good contributions and seem to have derived something from the course.

I. a catatonic schizophrenia - the type of mental disorder (functional psychosis, presumably) which is characterized by complete withdrawal into oneself. It is a dissociation from one's environment. all schizophrenia involves withdrawal.

b. anxiety state - a neurosis which results in the victim being unable to control or face anxiety. ~~Results in~~

c. depression - a healthy channeling of undesir-able impulses acc. to Klein

X d. conation -

X e. permissiveness - a 'jelly fish' sort of attitude toward ~~one~~ children and behavior conflicts.

f. paranoia - a psychosis which is characterized by an elaborate, skillful delusion of persecution.

g. fixation - an unhealthy attachment to another person or idea. Undesirable dependence.

h. Carl Rogers - Father of Non-directive Counseling.

i. Beers. - Mental hospital patient who began a crusade to clean up mental hospitals in Conn.

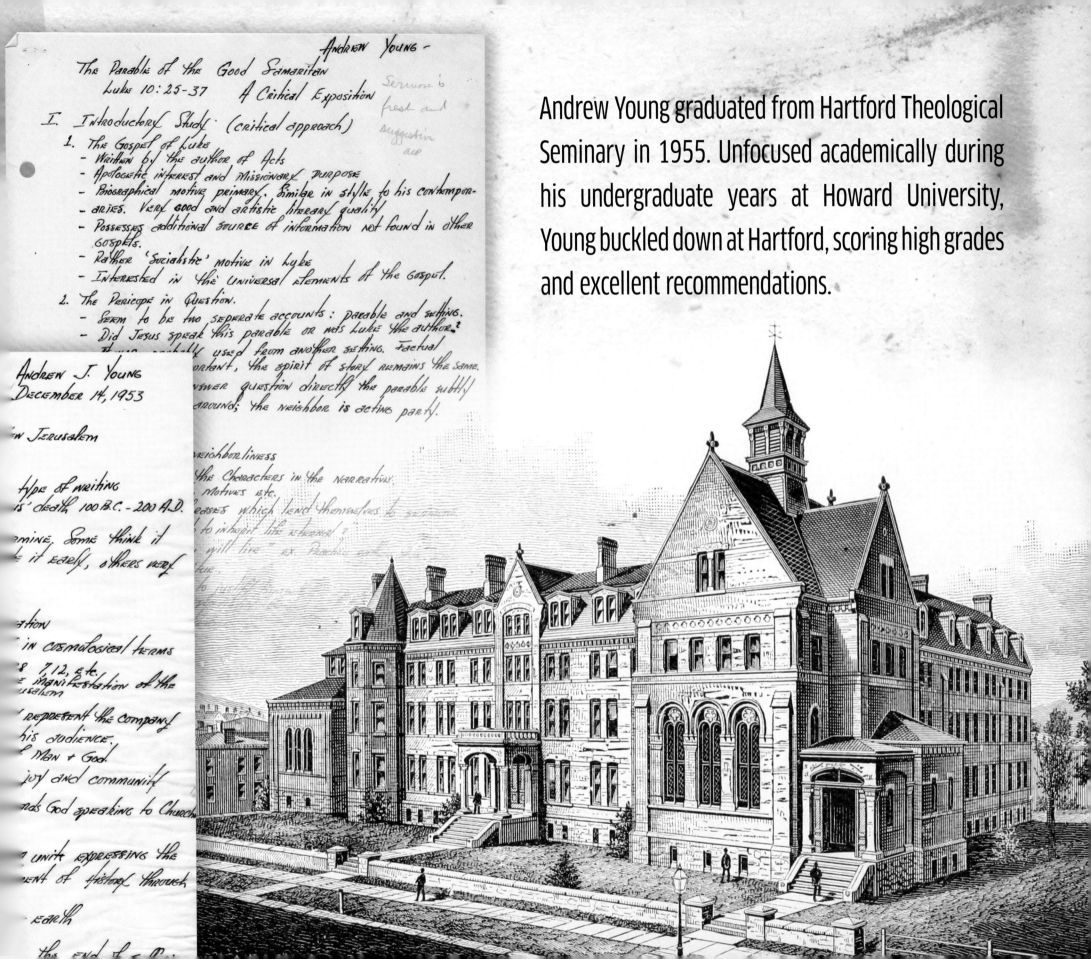

The Parable of the Good Samaritan
Luke 10:25-37   A Critical Exposition

Andrew Young

Sermon's fresh and suggestive ace

I. Introductory Study (critical approach)
  1. The Gospel of Luke
    - Written by the author of Acts
    - Apologetic interest and missionary purpose
    - Biographical motive primary. Similar in style to his contemporaries. Very good and artistic literary quality
    - Possesses additional source of information not found in other gospels.
    - Rather 'Socialistic' motive in Luke
    - Interested in the universal elements of the Gospel.
  2. The Pericope in Question.
    - Seem to be two separate accounts: parable and setting.
    - Did Jesus speak this parable or was Luke the author?

Andrew J. Young
December 14, 1953

Andrew Young graduated from Hartford Theological Seminary in 1955. Unfocused academically during his undergraduate years at Howard University, Young buckled down at Hartford, scoring high grades and excellent recommendations.

4 - Conflict was fed by Paul's eschatology
   Weiss   Vol II - Apocalyptic not central for Paul

5 - Conflict contd. to enter his life as a missionary
   11 Chap. I Cor.

6 - Paul's dialectical habit - putting things in terms of opposity-
   may be due to No. of things letters - relates to
   conflict
   - Paul flourished on disagreement, debate
   - virtue is in its clarity
   - weaknesses are temptation of exaggeration
          - so little ground for compromise   Relates past - indiv
univ   individualist   univ :: cosmic
Paul - Gal 5:25-26 - Paul an individualist - sees indiv in cosmic realm - Relates univ.
   - Paul was not totally framed by conflict, he was
     seeking an integrated approach to life which he found
     in Christ.

   Other Characteristics of Paul
   - No account of physical appearance
   - I Cor. 10:19 he quotes his accusers on "weak presence"
I Cor 12 - He was plagued with "thorn" - unstable psychic health
   - Yet he suffered great hardship & capably so
I Cor 11 - Natural man Paul was an egotist, (handy) often mention of boasting
Gal 6:12 - not very much of humor but there are some instances
   - Quite possible that Paul's contribution is exaggerated
     only a small portion of Mediterranean which Paul worked.
   - Must be reckoned as the outstanding exponent of
     the out going universal

Vol II p650 Weiss
   Personal grasp of rel is perennial fountain

[written vertically along spine:]
- Being baptized at Corinthians + Childhood is not
  enough to make a man a minister of Christ
                                        - George Fox

II. Paul's "Conversion"
1. - Paul never refers to conversion, he spoke of appearance,
     Revelation, New creation.
   - 3 ways 'conversion' does not apply
   1 - Not change from irreligious to religious man
   2 - not change from morally bad to morally good man
   3 - not change from one religion to another - no institutional
       change as such - Paul never foresaw Judaism rather
       he abandoned legalism for faith.

2. Preparation for this experience.
   * - in epistles Paul's outlook is dissatisfaction with himself
Rom 7 he would have thrown Judaism or law over rather than
       write so extensively in these areas
   - Rom 7 is generalized preaching rather than strictly
     autobiographical
   - intense passion for being right before God
   - he shared the temporary pessimism about man - depravity of man
   - Results 5-fold for Paul   no total
   1. Need for more than human power   Rather he taught the
   2. Repentance + Forgiveness in the   total inadequacy before
      frame of the law are not enough   God.
      - men need new motivation and   Original Sin passage
        center of life   of Adam's Fall not in O.T.
   3. Dissatisfaction led him to search   but from the pessimistic
      for radically new outlook on life   2nd Esdras &
      - new relationship central in his thought Paul argued for universal
      - if this is coupled with Paul's unstable temperament Sin not original Sin
        you see this preparation for this experience   Rom. 5:12

3. The nature of his central Religious experience
   - look to see if every reference to conversion is not
     related to his vocation
   - Paul talks of experiences in vocational terms but when he
     talks to them men must accept faith in Spirit which bears
     fruit in love - Heart of Pauline Theology

Andrew J. Young
November 23, 1953
New Testament - 58

Good!
acl

Hebrews 11:39 - 12:2   A Cloud of Witnesses

I. Introduction and Critical Background

A. General Background
- Purpose, date, and authorship unknown, but it is definitely not Pauline.
- First Christian Philosophy of Religion, and also a study in Comparative Religion (e.g. Christianity and Judaism)
- Judaism is the stepping stone to Christianity, which is God's final revelation.
- Argument is "a fortiori" or "How much more"
- Hellenistic world view incorporated with Jewish tradition.
- "Summum Bonum" is Draw near to God. It is therefore a liturgical or worship centered epistle.
- Greek is of superior quality to any in the New Testament.

B. ~~Theme or~~ Specific passage 11:39 - 12:2
- This is the beginning of the illustrative and practical material which follows the main argument.
- The analogy of the arena makes reference to Greek Games and is also found in Paul.
- Division of this passage is questionable but 11:39-'12:2 is a good preaching unit.
- Verse 11:39 is a summary of foregoing material & ~~introduction~~ to the illustration
- Faith is ~~an~~ natural quality for Hebrews. Different than in Paul

JEAN

EVANGELISCHES HEIM
RIED IM INNKREIS

Wed. Noon

Hi!
We had a very nice trip back in the jeep - it bumped too much to sleep but Rev. whatshisname kept it pretty jolly with jokes + some good stuff on China -. I certainly enjoyed being in your camp. I envy you in many respects + though I still think separation is miserable I hope its been worthwhile to both of us + to our relationship in the future.
I'm sorry about the attitude I brought but I feel a lot better about it now but I hope you understood. Even though my actions didn't seem to hurt you, I was pretty upset by them - not guilty feeling, just disappointed that I could act in such a weak & animal fashion. It wasn't fun!
We got back about 9:00 + went to work only to find that there are 2 shifts so we will be working until 6 unless Dick gets sore. I sure find it hard getting back into the swing of things. I was so tired I couldn't eat lunch so I drank my soup + came home. After this I'll nap for 10-15 min. It's amazing though how near we are to being finished with the diggings. We start pouring the basement foundation after lunch then in the morning we will finish cleaning up some of the caved in places + that's that. You really get a feeling of accomplishment.
I got a nice letter from Mother today - she said to be on look out for a money-order-. That'll sure help. If you haven't written Sister ask about approx. costs of the trip etc.
So long, going to sleep. Ich Liebe Dich!
Amerel, Andrew
Hello to Hans, Joe, Allen, Stanley, Vlado etc.

Miss Jean Childs
Lager Asten 117
Baarrack 12
Bei Linz/Donau
Ober Österreich

c/o B.S.C. Internat'l
Work Camp

RIEDER VOLKSFEST

Republik Österreich

HOTEL DE L'EUROPE
98, Boulevard de Magenta
(Entre les Gares du Nord et de l'Est)
PARIS (X°)
Direction : DEFFEIN   R. C. Seine 351.856
Tél. : NORD 25-82
Dernier Confort   ASCENSEUR

Relevé ne constituant pas acquit

M.   Childs et M. Young
App¹ N°   27 et 22
Mois de   3 sept 53

Report...				Total.........	
...ment..	3 nights	" 22	500	Taxe.........	1500
...euner..	3 nights	" 27	818	Majoration......	2454
				Débours.......	
...e					
...ter				Total général ..	3954

NOTA. - Les locations sont faites à la journée et les notes sont payables chaque semaine sur présentation.
Les Chambres occupées après 12 heures sont comptées pour une nouvelle journée.
Les Chèques ne sont pas acceptés en payment des notes (Chèques are not taken in payment of bills).

PRIÈRE DE LAISSER LA CLEF AU BUREAU AVANT LE DÉPART

Say it in
young
GERMA

A COMPREHENSIVE AND UP-TO-
CONVERSATIONAL GUIDE FOR AM
TOURISTS AND STUDENTS

✓ Accurate
idiomatic
✓ Thorough
indexed

SHOPPING
RAILROAD

Say
GER

A COMPREHENSIV
CONVERSATIONAL G
TOURISTS AN

SHOPPING
RAILROAD
THEATRE
FOOD · ETC.

This Book
Only 50¢

I made it to Marion, Alabama, and I found my way to the house where they said, I'll get my instructions. And I go in to a wonderful family—husband and wife, they're both members of the church and had businesses.

They had graduated too from a school in Marion, just like my parents had graduated from Straight College in New Orleans, part of the American Missionary Association. When I get there, I see a Bible open and it's underlined. So, I started looking through it and looking at the passages that are underlined, and I said, "These are some of my favorite passages. Whose Bible is this?"
"This is my daughter's Bible."

Then I said, "Who's the swimmer?"—there's a senior lifesaving certificate on the wall. She said, "That's my daughter." I say, "The same daughter reads the Bible and swims?" And I said, "And here's a basketball letter. She played basketball?" The parents said yeah, she's an all-around girl.

I still knew nothing else about the daughter except that she had taken a course in the New Testament nonviolence at Manchester College in Indiana. And I had been to Manchester College as part of my travels, and I knew some people there. So I decided that the Lord sent me to Marion to marry this woman.
I was so confident. See, this was God-ordained. When she came home, I went around and knocked on the front door. She was around the back. I go to the back gate and there is this beautiful little girl. Cutoff blue jeans and sweatshirt, these long plats. And she's milking this cow. And I thought it was the most beautiful picture in the world.

Stupid me. I went back to my car to get my camera, and she thought I was making fun of her. She stopped milking and came toward me and her first words were, "Get out of my way. If my mother didn't need this milk to make butter, I'd throw it in your ugly face." I had made the wrong approach. But I still thought the only reason I could have been sent to Marion, Alabama, was to marry this woman. All my life was before me. But it had a rocky start. But I was so determined that it didn't matter whether she loved me. What she thought of me didn't matter because she was going to be my wife.

We lasted for forty years before she died of cancer.
Jean was the only black student at Manchester College, and in the summer of 1953, the Church of the Brethren had summer programs to help refugees in Europe, and they gave her a scholarship. I wasn't gonna let her go to Europe by herself. I was in seminary then and I had four jobs. I was washing dishes, working at the bookstore, wrapping books, and selling them. There was an apartment right across the street from the campus with mostly senior citizens and they needed somebody to fire their furnace and empty the ashes and keep the halls clean. I had enough money and I called the program and asked if I could pay my own way.

I don't think it was $350, but we went by an old cattle boat and it took us eleven days to get to Europe. Nobody but students and cows on the boat. We spent the whole summer in Europe. Jean said they want Europeans to meet more African American students, so you should not go to the same camp I'm going to. She was in one part of Austria and I was in another part. She was working with children. I was building a refugee settlement house. We had to dig a twenty-foot foundation. There was no heavy equipment. We had to dig with shovels and roll the dirt up out of the hole in our wheelbarrow. That's what I did for six weeks. I probably have not been in as good shape ever in my life.

We got a chance to see pretty much all of Europe from LeHavre all the way down to Rome. Jean's sister was working in Berlin, with the YMCA, so we went behind the Iron Curtain to visit her. Then we went back to LeHavre. Jean provided me with my first nonviolent experience and my first international experience.

February 7, 1954

Dear Folks,

The semester is underway and things are _____ all _____ that is all but one and since I am required to take it I must bear it.

My eyes have been bothering me quite a bit here lately. I plan to have them examined. I have been having headaches and my eyes burn but I wanted to make sure it wasn't just a lack of sleep.

I got a letter from the A.M.A. They asked if I was interested in a Church and Community house in McIntosh, Ga. The guy is coming up here. _____ would _____ _____ to talk with him but that I was more interested in foreign missions at present. It will depend on which _____ a job I feel I can accomplish more in. There are so many decisions involved right along through here. I'll have to be awful sure I'm making the right one for I do believe that there is only one right one.

Its kinda hard to answer your question about I Cor. 15. I really have given little or no thought to such questions. For me they are of

secondary importance. What is important is that God loves and cares for men in life and death. I can only obey His law in life and die with faith that he will do what is best and true with my soul. I don't care what it may be.

I would not interpret scripture in the literal, word for word manner of your friend. Its only been a hundred years or so that man has thought in strictly rational + literal terms. In Jesus time + in the New Testament, language and thought were more poetic and a truth was expressed but not defined so precisely as we would today. Hence the great truths of Jesus are parables + we know Paul expressed things such as the Church being the body of Christ etc. We had to live in the spirit of the Gospel and not according to the Bible as law. Christ is the fulfillment of the law. We live by the spirit of the Bible.

You can't argue _____ with a person like that. In fact you can't argue religion. We all have faith in God but I express it in a way true to my personality and you must do the same. We are _____ _____ _____ _____

Why don't you ask Dick about it. Its hard to write what you mean.

Tell everyone hello —

Love,
Andrew

Left: Andrew Young during his ordination 1955.
Central Congregational Church, New Orleans, Louisiana

TESTING FAITH

Top: The Young Wedding Party in Marion, Alabama. June 7, 1954, From L to R Cora C. Moore, *(Maid of Honor)* Sister, Tom Dent *(Best man)* Walter Young *(brother)*

Left: Jean and Andrew Young cutting the cake.

Right: Andrew Young marries Jean Childs.

After spending the summer in Europe, we came back and decided that Jean would go back to Manchester College and finish. We'd get married after her graduation in Marion.

I went back to seminary and then realized I was about to be assigned to Thomasville and Beachton, Georgia. That was perfect for Jean because her hometown was three thousand people. Thomasville at that time was about ten thousand and Beachtown was about a hundred and fifty people.

Passing through Atlanta, I ran into Maynard Jackson's grandfather and told him I was going down to Thomasville. And he said, would you help us run a voter registration drive down there? I said, I'd be glad to. I really didn't think anything of it. This was 1955. When we agreed, he said he would come down there and kick it off on a Sunday. The Saturday before John Wesley Dobbs came to Thomasville, Jean and I went to Albany, Georgia, which is fifty miles away. We decided to take the shortcut through the back roads. We came back through Moultrie, Georgia, and we came around a curve just south of Moultrie in a little town called Doe Run, Georgia, in our little Nash Rambler.

Lo and behold, it seemed like a thousand Klansmen were on the road. They were in full Klan regalia. And that was about ten miles outside of Thomasville. I assume that they were coming to Thomasville and since they hadn't been there before, I figured it must have had something to do with our voter registration drive. We passed by without incident and when we got back home, it was confirmed that the Klan had been gathering from all over southwest Georgia to come to Thomasville to intimidate us.

I had been reading Reinhold Niebuhr, and I told Jean that I didn't want to run from these people. I reflected back to earlier when Jean and I were driving down from Hartford to Thomasville and stopped at the Coney Island Amusement Park in New York City. We went to the shooting gallery and Jean shot sixteen of the twenty moving targets and I shot eighteen.

So when we got home that night after seeing the Klan, I told Jean, "If the Klan comes they are going to try to intimidate. If they come, I am going to go downstairs and confront them outside in the front yard. I want you to sit in the upstairs window with the rifle. When I identify the leader, I am going to tell him that my wife has a rifle trained right between his eyes. If we do this, we can deal with them from a position of strength."

Jean looked at me hard and said she wasn't going to touch that gun. I told her that she was a great shot—as I had seen at Coney Island. I said, "Baby, that's the Ku Klux Klan." And she said, "Yeah, and you're supposed to be a preacher. And if you ever forget that under that sheet is the heart of a child of God, then you need to quit preaching." She said, "If you don't believe in the cross and the resurrection, you need to find something else to do."

I was really angry because she was obviously so much more spiritual than me. But it did make me think. And I called one of the elders in the community. We arranged to talk to the mayor, who ran the local hardware store. We told him about the Klan, and what he did was one of my most valuable lessons in the movement.

He didn't say anything to us. He picked up the phone and called the plant managers at Flowers Bakery and Sunnyland packing company. I realized that the ones who call the shots are the businesspeople. It takes 50 percent to get rid of a sheriff or a mayor, but businesspeople are much more sensitive. They will feel the trouble if there's just a 10 percent drop in their earnings. So they told him that he was right to call them. And their suggestion was that he let the Klan meet on the courthouse steps, but that he surround the courthouse steps with his deputies and not let the Klan march in the black community. And then on Sunday make sure that the deputies are keeping anybody from interfering with our mass rally that John Wesley Dobbs was speaking at. It worked out perfectly, but normally we don't think of the spiritual answer first.

I thought of my own hide. I'd seen the Klan before, I'd been around a Klan before, but I wasn't afraid though neither did I have a martyr complex. And I don't think Jean did either, but it let me know that the first choice we usually make involves violence and even self-defensive violence is not your best choice.

The Board of Home Missions
— OF THE —
Congregational Christian Churches
DISTRICT OF THE SOUTHEAST
P. O. BOX 957
GREENSBORO, N. C.

REV. J. T. STANLEY
SUPERINTENDENT
RES.: 1712 McCONNELL RD.
PHONE 3-4531

EXTENSION WORKER:

March 16, 1954

Mr. Andrew Young
Hartford Seminary Foundation
55 Elizabeth Street
Hartford 5, Connecticut

Dear Mr. Young:

I have returned to your letter of March 10 after having had a delightful visit with Central Church in New Orleans and a most delightful dinner visit with your parents and others at your home. A very good friend of yours, Miss Louise Childs, was also a guest in the home, and was present at each of our services during the preaching mission.

In answer to a portion of your letter I think that probably the McIntosh situation should be dropped from your thinking. I am reasonably certain that our A.M.A. officials feel that the McIntosh job is of such complicated magnitudes that a person of some type of experience in this type of community affairs should be considered. I do wish that you would give serious consideration to the Thomasville-Beachton situation. In fact you were in the background of my thinking when I described to the two churches the kind of person I would like to recommend to them for leadership. I received today a letter from one of these churches urging that I do all that I possibly can to send to them the right sort of young man. The church wants to know as early as possible what to expect so that they can be prepared to make whatever provisions are necessary for the home life and comfort of the coming minister.

This is a situation that would have no precedents about which you would need to be concerned. The field is almost totally unexplored and would be ready to move in any direction behind leadership in which the two churches would have confidence. The situations also are almost wholly undeveloped so that you would have the equivalent of almost a new field, especially at Thomasville. It is my further opinion that you would have the ability, the tact, and the enthusiasm which would make the work in this situation a success. As I have said previously, if you consider this work seriously, we will give you every possible encouragement toward making it a satisfactory experience. So that I may know how to proceed with reference to the churches, I will appreciate it very much if you will let me hear from you as early as possible, please.

Very cordially yours,

J. Taylor Stanley
Superintendent

JTS/jh

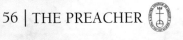

---

55 Elizabeth Street
Hartford, Connecticut
March 20, 1954

Rev. J. Taylor Stanley
P.O. Box 957
Greensboro, N. C.

Dear Rev. Stanley,

Thanks very much for your letter of March 16th concerning the churches in Thomasville and Beachton. I find it very awkward to give any final answer at the present time since my plans are so uncertain. I will say that this is the most interesting and appealing situation of the offers I have recieved. It is the type of thing that both Jean and I would be interested in. I would like to have some time to get my personal affairs in order before making any sort of commitment.

At present the big problem is my graduation. I would prefer to finish my seminary training before accepting a call to a church. I am trying to make arrangements to finish by going to Union this summer. I am hoping to live with an aunt in New York in order to lighten the financial burden. This way I could begin in September with a church. If I came to Thomasville-Beachton this summer, I would have to spend another semester in school. This would hinder any progress we could make in the churches during the summer, by my absence for (5) five months. I would like your opinion on the problem however. If there are any suggestions that you could make toward a better solution, I would appreciate it.

This decision means that I would have to accept the churches on your recommendation, but I have no objections to that. At the end of the summer I might not be as optomistic as I am now. Three (3) months is just enough time to work yourself into dificulty by trying to rush the program. Prehaps I could visit the church on the way to summer school, provided I can find a way to get home.

The only important question I have in regard to these churches is whether there is a large enough un-churched population for the church to grow on. That was the problem in Marion and I should imagine it would be in many communities. Congregationalism does have a lot to offer that the other denominations don't, but denominational loyalty means more than meaningful Christianity to most of the people. I would really hate to have the church grow at the expense of other churches anyway. The housing project could be a good source of membership, provided it's residents are from other communities.

I hope I have made my predicament understandable. I will keep in touch with you and will try to make some definite decision as soon as possible. I will be looking forward to any suggestions or information as you see fit to offer.

Sincerely,

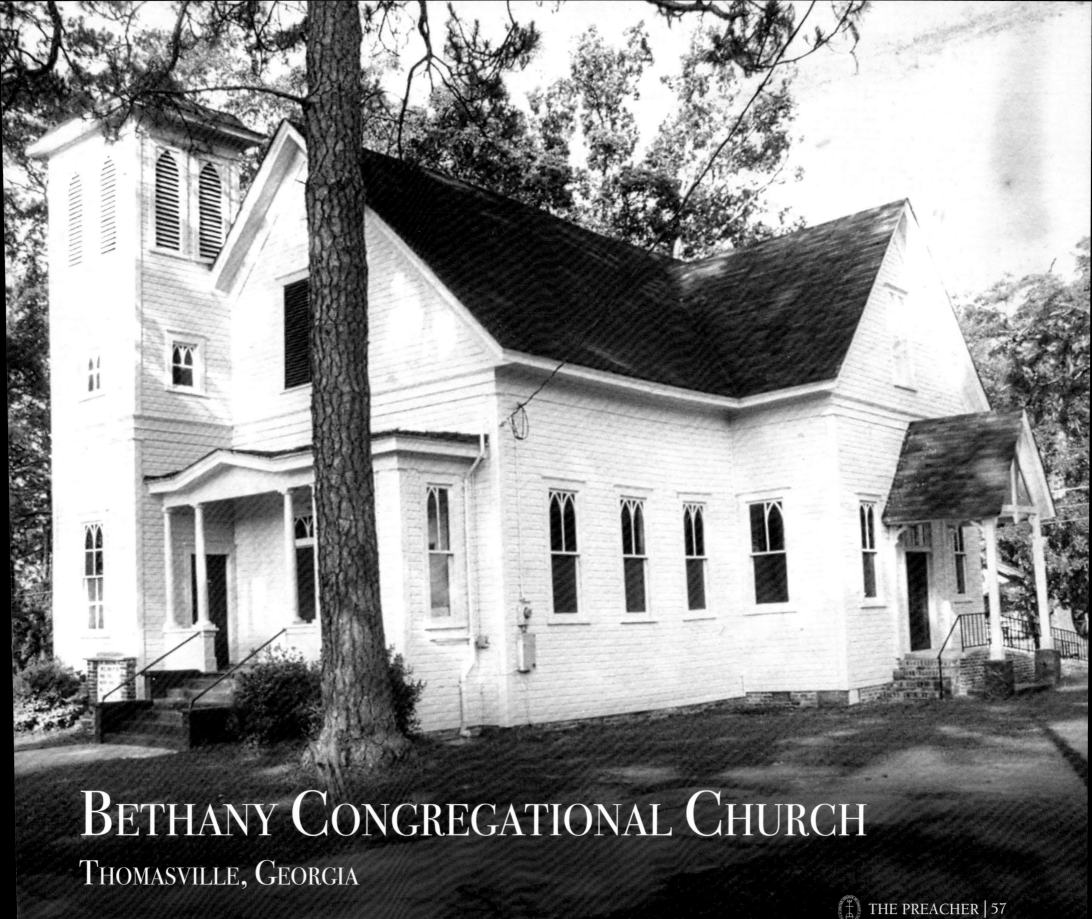

BETHANY CONGREGATIONAL CHURCH
THOMASVILLE, GEORGIA

John Wesley Dobbs came down, and I'll never forget his sermon was, "Stick with this blue-eyed boy, but watch him."

The other thing that was unusual for me at that time was that he said now we're voting Republican down here. I said, well, I'm a Democrat. He said, you can be a Democrat up in New England, but down here you with Eisenhower, I said, might I ask why? He said, well, there are no white Republicans and very few black ones. So, if there's a nomination for a federal judge or a government position, they are much more likely to ask us than ask somebody from another state. That turned out to be one of the wisest decisions we made because every judge—this was 1955, 1956—when the civil rights movement got aggressive and active in 1960 with the sit-ins and the freedom rides, every time we won a case, it was before one of the Republican-appointed judges.

And the reason was that black people had nominated them. He said if Adlai Stevenson is elected, Senators Richard Russell of Georgia and James Eastland of Mississippi will nominate the judges. He said, if Eisenhower is elected, they will ask us who we would like to see as federal judges. So every case won in the civil rights movement was before judges like Frank Johnson in Montgomery, John Minor Wisdom in Louisiana, and Brian Simpson, who decided my case in Jacksonville.

All of those ended up being landmark cases and the judges were all Eisenhower appointees. In spite of how divided we are today, I don't like one party to be alienated from the other. We said later on in the movement that we have no permanent friends, no permanent enemies, only permanent interests.

ANDREA
AUGUST 3, 1955

Left: Andrew Young feeding Andrea 1955.

Middle: Thanksgiving in Atlanta 1960's, Andrew Young, Lisa *(4)* Andrea *(7)* Daisy Young *(back)* Andrew Young, Sr. *(back right)* Paula *(newborn)* Jean Young.

Right: Andrew Young, Jean and Andrea, Thomasville, Georgia 1955.

While we were in Thomasville, I got invited to Florida to do Bible study by the same National Council of Churches that had invited Nicholas Hood out to Texas with me in 1951.

It was almost 10 years later that they invited me to come down to middle Florida and lead Bible study. When I finished, they asked if I would be interested in a job. The NCC problem was that there were six hundred executives, and the only one who was black was in race relations. The NCC wanted somebody black who was not in the department of race relations. So, they had a vacancy for the department of youth work and asked me if I would be willing to come to New York.

It was a wonderful opportunity, because it got me out of the South, but I really didn't want to leave Thomasville. I was just getting settled in there even though I had almost been put out. The conference superintendent said, "Look, I know you like it here. And we like you here. You all have done a good job of fixing up this house and church but now if you move on, we can bring in somebody else. And it would be a very good opportunity for you to go to New York."

Well, I went to New York as the associate director of the department of youth work. And one of my jobs was as associate producer of a film, Look Up and Live, which ran on Sunday mornings at 10 a.m. It was an attempt to talk about life in secular terms but asserting and affirming religious and spiritual values. And it gave us an opportunity for a maximum amount of creativity.

This was 1957. Jazz was just beginning to blossom, but the Protestant churches understood jazz, in the context of the African American creative bent. They saw jazz and the spirituals as religious music if you focused it that way. So, we were trying to get people to listen to music—this so-called new music in the 1950s.

We had The Modern Jazz Quartet, Dave Brubeck, Billy Taylor, Maya Angelo, Odetta. We were very heavy on folk songs. We had a short dramatic series with Dick van Dyke. It was an experimental attempt to find something that would give young people an additional perspective on their lives.

That turned out to be a very good experience for me. Jean and I stayed there for four years. In addition to what I did culturally, with films and music, I was also involved with international activities of the church. One of the experiences that has come back to help me was in 1960. I went to Geneva, Switzerland, for an international youth conference. They needed a colored face so they asked if I was ordained and if I was would I mind serving communion? One of the people I served communion to was Princess Beatrix of Holland. Jumping way ahead, that became even more significant because by the time we brought the Olympics to Atlanta, Princess Beatrix was Queen Beatrix. And when she visited Atlanta, I was the mayor, and she remembered the youth conference in Switzerland.

But I had a number of opportunities to travel, to be involved religiously with people in Latin America or Europe. That was part of my religious education. When I became mayor of Atlanta, all of these were resources that I was able to plug back into and between the relationships that I had through the churches of Europe and the religious hierarchy and the Coca-Colas of Atlanta, it made me quite comfortable in trying to deal with the rest of the world.

Left: Beachton Community Church, one of Reverend Young's first church assignments.

Left Middle: Family picture with Andrea, Lisa and Paula Young.

Far Right: Andrew Young Jr., Andrew Young IV (*grandson*), Abigail Young (*granddaughter*), Andrew "Bo" Young III revisiting the Thomasville church.

"Voter Education in Tennessee then Georgia."

One of the key elements in fighting for civil rights was training in it, particularly in nonviolence. Throughout the South, citizenship schools, spearheaded by Septima Poinsette Clark, sprang up to teach nonviolent strategies. Andrew Young, pictured with "Big Lester" and his daughters Lisa and Andrea, was a regular attendee and trainer.

WE'RE TOO YOUNG TO REGISTER...

....WHAT'S YOUR EXCUSE?

Segregation Must GO!
Do Not be a Second Class Citizen

Do NOT Attend THE SEGREGATED

Mississippi State Fair
FOR NEGROES
October 16 - 18, 1961
Jackson Branch NAACP
Jackson Youth Council
Tougaloo College Chapter
Campbell College Chapter
Miss. Conference of Branches NAACP
Jackson Non-Violent Movement

Highlander Reports

28th ANNUAL REPORT   October 1, 1959 - Sept. 30, 1960

HIGHLANDER FOLK SCHOOL
MONTEAGLE, TENNESSEE

. . . Panel of Consultants at Highlander Workshop

The democratic initiative, so recently seized and powerfully demonstrated by Southern college students, has brought an upsurg-ing of hopeful vitality throughout the liberal South—good news for

The goals in sight are still to be reached. What the coming year will bring at Highlander can be predicted in terms of a sched-ule of workshops and projects, as is listed on page 4; however, whatever is to happen will be determined by new sights of con-

Septima Poinsette Clark, known as the "Mother of the Movement," was a pioneer of grassroots citizenship education. She conducted workshops at Tennessee's Highlander Folk School, a grassroots education center dedicated to social justice.

Left: Andrew Young teaches a class on voter literacy.
Top Right: Dorchester Citizenship School.
Left middle: Participants learn the process of voting.
Right Bottom: Dorothy Cotton and team training.

"The Revolutionary Power in The Gospel May Well Be Our Final, Only Hope . . ."

Hope In The Quest For Economic Justice

by Andrew Young

The Liturgical Week program at Milwaukee, reported on the previous page, was marked by a number of significant addresses, among them one by Andrew J. Young, Executive Vice-President of the Southern Christian Leadership Conference. A condensation of his presentation follows.

YOU called on a pretty hopeless brother to talk about signs of hope in the quest for a more equitable distribution of wealth and the world's resources. The more I began to reflect on what's really going on in this world—frankly, the more discouraged I got. But I've been looking for just those few little candles and sparkles of light in the midst of what seems to be a very dark situation. And while I have no particular hope at present, for some strange reason beyond my earthly hope, beyond my understanding and my own resources, there is somehow a confidence and a hope that comes from God which makes it possible to go on.

Quickly, let me see if I can get you just about as discouraged as I am. In 1950, the poor were 60 per cent of the world's population and received 13.2 per cent of the world's income. In 1964, the poor were down to 11.1 per cent of income. In 1950, the rich were 40 per cent—receiving 86.8 per cent of the world's income. In 1964, they control even more—88.9 per cent. Whether you look at home or abroad the rich are getting richer and the poor are getting poorer. It's enough to make you ask the question—Is the earth really the Lord's and the fullness thereof? Because when I look around the world it seems as though it belongs to the Rockefellers and not to the people of God.

The statistics that I just called off could be multiplied and reaffirmed in terms of the birth rate, in terms of health services, in terms of educational opportunities — almost any category you want to choose. All of us as Americans have to think of ourselves as the rich of the world when we're looking at the world situation.

But black folks still seem to be living in a different era from most Americans. We're re-entering the 1870's rather than the 1970's. You know, we were almost free once. After the Civil War we did get the right to vote. We took over County Court Houses across the south, half of the state legislature in South Carolina. We did have a senator in Mississippi who was black. Yet in a matter of ten short years we were run out of politics — almost the same way we're being run out now. The civil rights act passed in 1875 was better, on its face, than the civil rights act passed in 1964.

Stacking the Court

But a Supreme Court appointed by a Republican administration declared the act unconstitutional. There was a deal made in the 1870's between the rich Republicans and the racists of the South. The racists in the South got control of the politics and the niggers, and Republicans in the north got control of the money. That same kind of deal Nixon and Thurmond made last August. The South once again appoints the likes of Justice Haynsworth to the Supreme Court—shifting a balance of 5-4 that probably gave us blacks the only possible governmental chance for survival, because we could never count on the executive branch or the Congress very much. This stacking of the courts gives the South a new political power, protection of its racism by the Federal judiciary.

What you see here and around the world is a destruction of the forces of reason. The great statesman that united Nigeria and gave it its vision of being the greatest nation in Africa was assassinated. Colonels took over, men who, whatever their nationality, are notoriously devoid of statesmanship. (If there is anything worse than the generals, it is the colonels.) So tribal conflicts, which one suspects were instigated by oil interests, will keep a nation divided into Nigeria and Biafra and a people confused and, once confused, thereby controlled, thereby poor.

tion against nation. It's really rich against poor. It's really government not by national government but international policy determined by American corporations and their puppets. In a high-class way we're milking the economies of these other countries. In fact stealing from them the God-given resources that they possess. The American investments in Africa have brought a 23 per cent return. In Asia a 36 per cent return. In Latin America a 12 per cent return. And yet when I pick up Fortune magazine and look at the profits of the 500 top corporations in terms of the American operation very few if any of them reach 10 per cent.

The Communist Fizzle

There was once a hope that international communism would liberate the poor, bridge the gap between the haves and the have-nots. Yet all over Latin America, Communist parties are in fact working against revolution and radical social change. Those who have come, rather naively, to hope in Marxism and Leninism find themselves rudely awakened by the fact that even communism is enjoying a status of wealth. Communism wants to avoid not only war with the United States—but the risk of having to share the resources of the Communist world with any more Cubas.

Where do we go? Where is there any hope? I'd like to hope in the students, but I've seen two generations of students cop out over the civil rights movement. The students of the '60's—some 20,000 strong went to jail across the South, committed to patterns of radical direct action— as soon as those poverty program jobs came along they traded their overalls for attache cases and went along with the Man. They, too, got hooked on a consumer economy and once you get in debt—once you get a charge account, put a down payment on an automobile or on a house, you can forget it. The giant consumer economy has even created a kind of consumer slavery amongst the affluent that makes them as controllable as the poor are controllable.

But every now and then there is a little candle in the garden. And I've seen one or two of those candles in the last few months. God knows how long they'll burn. The irony of this whole thing is that America, from top to bottom, is not as corrupt, vicious, murderous as its systems and its institutions would make it seem. Our government and corporations are being dominated by a few people who let greed and ignorance run their lives, who have so little vision that they can't see around the corner, much less the turn of the next decade. I've seen for the first time the possibility of an attack upon that power elite, which keeps us and most of the world confused and enslaved.

The Southern Picture

Mendel Rivers in South Carolina is one of the men who dominate our congressional committees, who sees to it that half of our Federal budget by virtue of congressional seniority goes into foolishness and destructiveness. Yet it dawned on me that Mendel Rivers is elected from a congressional district that is 45 per cent black. If those black voters ever decide to vote, you may not have a revolution in America but you'll have a qualitative structural reform of the Congress which might liberate a good portion of that $80 billion war budget. If we could just liberate $20 billion of it a year we could probably, with our present technological capability, wipe out poverty here — and make a good start in becoming brothers to the Third World.

We could also un-elect Richard Russell from my home state of Georgia, who sends tremendous military contracts to Lockheed in Atlanta. You remember they recently got a $3.1 billion contract to build 120 C58 transports—and then all of a sudden the cost grew to $5 billion in some unexplained way. Also remember that the poor people in Mississippi and in the child's development group of Mississippi had their government

(Continued on page 11)

HOPE IN THE QUEST

(Continued from page 5)

Headstart contract revoked because of so-called fiscal irresponsibility. The $2 billion the Lockheed branch of the military establishment overspent on **one contract** was greater than the total amount of the poverty program in the United States from coast to coast.

People criticize the Southern Christian Leadership Conference by saying we're a southern organization; that we're afraid of the north and can't do anything in the cities. But we know where the problem in America lies and it still lies in the southeast. If you could ever get Lockheed to make subways and rapid transit systems instead of bombers you could solve most of the problems in the city. The main reason you can't get them to do that is because of the military mentality of those southern senators that dominate our Congress.

Unseating the "Unseatable"

We've seen that we can defeat this mentality. In Green County, Alabama, just a few weeks ago, black people showed the potential of taking over a county government. My prayer and my hope is that the 500 black nurses who recently won a strike in Mendel Rivers' district will devote the next two years of their lives trying to unseat him. You know we've never had a city anywhere in America where 500 people were committed to two years of consistent political activity. We can't give up on the system until we have at least fought it a little bit. These nurses finally saw the possibility of their own power in their own neighborhood. They watched the governor of the state of South Carolina go from being an oppressor (with his 1,500 National Guards) to a clown. Because they didn't curse the guard or throw bricks, but sang to them "who's making love to your old lady while you been out messing with us," refusing to hate, with their laughs and even love for their oppressors, for **one hundred and twenty days** they found a capacity for soul power they know to be revolutionary. They may make a revolution in the congressional district that will affect the status of the poor around the world.

We were able to get some enlightenment into brother Roger Blough of United States Steel, but only after we literally brought the economy of Birmingham to a halt. Frederick Douglass said a long time ago that this is a struggle to save black men's bodies and white men's souls. When the white poor and the black begin to really rear up and refuse to cooperate with the continued exploitation of the poor here and around the world —when they bring the economy to a sweeping halt, even for a minute—it's amazing how quick folk get religion.

The Lights Ahead

Perhaps there are many many candles—lit up people—but I know that their lives are as much in jeopardy as was Martin Luther King, or Bobby Kennedy or Tom Mboya. There has to be some political and economic action to keep them alive. We as a people in the eye of the dragon have to find a way to give them the kind of support that they need in order to survive.

Yet these are not the things that are concerning us. We've developed a mood of rebellion—a mood of being hip and with it and swinging. Our whole concept of revolution and social change is something rather avant garde. We are much more concerned about radical images than relevant images. We rebel against the church more strongly than we rebel against the Fascist government. We rebel against the very liberties that we reaffirm and celebrate.

There's no need talking with Latin-American peasants, or black peasants for that matter, about any kind of Marxist ideology or student revolutionary concept. If they don't understand the revolutionary content within the Gospel, they'll never understand anything. Even if you don't believe in it politically, just a sensible anthropology would be able to tell you that when you're dealing with the poor in the western hemisphere, it's a waste of time to fight the church—people's folk religion.

Soon one day—and I've heard that they're doing it already across Latin America—good, humble, poor Catholic women are going down to the town square with their madonnas—just like Cesar Chavez marched down California highways—reaffirming their faith in action. Literally celebrating their hope and their faith in God on the streets. This says that there's a revolutionary power in the Gospel which may well be our final and our only hope. Perhaps amid all of this darkness a chain of candles might come together that might light our way from one step to the next and lead us through this dark period to that day when the world's resources will be more adequately redistributed. ■

HOPE THROUGH RENEWAL

(Continued from page 8)

come out as surplus of silence, as the fruit of lived faith, of enduring intimacy.

PRAYER will not come about by default. It requires education, training, reflection, contemplation. It is not enough to join others; it is necessary to build a sanctuary within, brick by brick, instants of meditation, moments of devotion. This is particularly true at an age when overwhelming forces seem to conspire at destroying our ability to pray.

The relentless pursuit of our interests makes us oblivious of reality itself. Nothing we experience has value in itself; nothing counts unless it can be turned to our advantage, into a means for serving our self-interests.

The beginning of prayer is praise. The power of worship is song. First we sing, then we understand. First we praise, then we believe. Praise and song open eyes to the grandeur of reality that transcends the self. Song restores the soul; praise repairs spiritual deficiency.

While it is true that being human is gained and verified in relations between man and man, depth and authenticity of existence are disclosed in moments of worship.

Worship is more than paying homage. To worship is to join the cosmos in praising God. The whole cosmos, every living being sings, the Psalmists insist. Neither joy nor sorrow but song is the ground-plan of being. It is the quintessence of life. To praise is to call forth the promise and presence of the divine. We live for the sake of a song. We praise for the privilege of being.

"CHOOSE LIFE!" is the great legacy of the Hebrew Bible, and the cult of life is affirmed in contemporary theology. However, life is not a thing, static and final. Life means living, and in living you have to choose a road, direction, goals. Pragmatists who believed that life itself can provide us with the criteria for truth overlook the fact that inherent in life are also forces of suicide and destruction.

Just to be is a blessing. Just to live is holy. And yet, being alive is no answer to the problems of living. To be or not to be is **not** the question. The vital question is: how to be and how not to be?

The tendency to forget this vital question is the tragic disease of contemporary man, a disease

that may prove fata
To pray is **passionate**
urgency of this vita

Religious commi
ent of the social or
ment of existence, bu
being human, its ex
manifest in the socia

Religious existe
God. Yet to maint
knowing how to cr
are more numerous
character there is
devotion is really to
tion to assume tha
man. In order to be
human.

A person must
ways rise, he must
you are.

Well-trodden
are no easy ways,
What comes easy
tragic error to ass
our direction is
vertical. It is eithe
or fall.

THE tragedy of
out of the dim
abandoned the in
God can be patier
ished. Intimate in
can never remain
for grace or it is

At first men
taking counsel w
derstand one ano
between the gene
an abyss. The on
consult God be
another.

Prayer bring
erected between
God.

WE of this
severe case
the result of o
result God's d
lights?

Spiritual m
words are dilut
tions drained.

Is God to b

Is it not ma
hearts and min

This is an
out of God. W
night of the so
ciety. Together
society, we mus
truth of a livin
Blackout.

For the da
Our power is f
ness, for the d
in coming up
casional ways,
and radiance.

We are ca
preserve and
moments of r
pair and to w
be light. And

'CRISIS' IN LITURGY

(Continued from page 2)

newal is a serious matter. Too serious in its implications to be guided by sentimentality, nostalgia, fire-and-brimstone theology or an other-age oriented bureaucracy. "Let go, Father."

Mr. Colainni, a Catholic layman, is Executive Director of the U.S. Liturgical Conference whose annual meeting is reported on elsewhere in this issue.

FILL IN AND MAIL RIGHT NOW

TEMPO P.O. BOX 81, MADISO
NEW YORK,

Please enter my subscription for:
☐ 1 year, $3.50 ☐ 2 years, $6.00

Name

Address

City State

Payment in advance, please ☐ Check

(For foreign postage, add $1.00 per year)

December 1, 1960

Mr. Andrew Young
National Council of Churches
475 Riverside Dr.
New York 27, New York

Dear Andy,

You may recall my mentioning the interesting out-
come of tape recorded material in work with delinquents
--extraordinary insight seems to dawn. As a result of
hearing exerpts from these tapes, one of our students
worked out a remarkable service of worship alternating
between classic prayers and the words of the youth.
Wouldn't it be of value to make a tape which would
give the raw material and then the worship which evolved?
I was thinking a player could be set up at St. Louis
for those who would elect to hear it. If this doesn't

---

ury 18, 1961

ans Hofmann
ancis Avenue
idge 38, Massachusetts

Dr. Hofmann:

hat our General Assembly and Christmas Holidays are over and we
nto the New Year, my attention turns more specifically to Youth
on. I trust that your ideas continue to "boil over" on the sub-
of Christian Faith and Adolescent Development. We are anxiously
ing your presentations.

lleagues in Youth Work are so excited about your topics and their
late relevance to our work, that we have already raised questions
publication of this material. I recall your mentioning the fact
ome of this is already scheduled for release in book form. I
appreciate a word from you concerning this.

e arranged for you to leave Boston on Monday, February 13 at
. This flight (American Airlines - 49 Touristar Jet) will
Chicago, O'Hare Airport at 9:25 and you will transfer to
an Airlines flight # 597 and arrive St. Louis at 12:36 p.m..
e scheduled your return to Boston for Thursday afternoon.
an be changed if you like. Your tickets will be forwarded short

---

HARVARD UNIVERSITY

UNIVERSITY PROJECT ON
RELIGION AND MENTAL HEALTH

45 FRANCIS AVENUE
CAMBRIDGE 38, MASSACHUSETTS

7 July 1960   UN 45985

Mr. Andrew J. Young
Associate Executive
Department of Youth Work
National Council of the Churches of Christ in the U.S.A.
475 Riverside Drive
New York 27, New York

Dear Mr. Young:

Thank you very much for your letter of June 30, 1960. I have cleared
the dates on my calendar and will be happy to be with you in St. Louis
February 13-15. I have spoken with Ed Spradling concerning how these
three days could be best structured. I am very much interested in the
questions and topics which you mentioned, and I would suggest that they
be dealt with in the following way.

I would give three main presentations on the general theme of the
critical function of the Christian faith in the adolescent's development
of personality. I would relate my thoughts especially to the particular
situation which the American church and culture create for young people
and would deal with youth response to the Christian faith in our culture.
We could possibly start off in the morning with my lecture, then break
off into small discussion groups, and later bring questions and suggestions arising from the small group discussions to the plenum where I
would deal with them again. Otherwise, my presentation could be held
in the morning, followed by a recess, and then group meetings and
general assemblies could be held in the later afternoon.

The topics of my three lectures would be the Crucifixion, Resurrection,
and Pentecost, since I feel that the theological impact of these events
speaks best to the major problems which arise in relating the core of
the question of faith to contemporary American youth. I certainly will
address myself to some descriptive analysis of American youth and youth
culture and an evaluation of the church's present ministries since I am
very much interested in these questions and have done some thinking on
them.

I am agreeable to informal and personal contacts so that the conference participants can get to know me. As I told you over the telephone

---

HARVARD UNIVERSITY

UNIVERSITY PROJECT ON
RELIGION AND MENTAL HEALTH

45 FRANCIS AVENUE
CAMBRIDGE 38, MASSACHUSETTS

September 23, 1960

Mr. Andrew J. Young
National Council of the Churches of Christ
475 Riverside Drive
New York 27, New York

Dear Mr. Young:

February 14 - 16 are clear on my calendar, and I shall be happy
to be with you in St. Louis at that time. I look forward to seeing
you sometime soon.

Sincerely yours,

Hans Hofmann

Hans Hofmann

PS

---

with your schedule. We would very much like to have you with
us for planning on the 13th, but definitely we will need you
for the ending of the St. Louis meeting on the 16th. This
is very important.

If any damage has been done please let us know and we'll
do our best to apply the patch work now.

May I again apologize for my mistake. My trip to Europe
at that time seemed to monopolize my thinking.

Thank you for your consideration and cooperation. I look
forward to our St. Louis meeting.

Sincerely,

Andrew J. Young
Associate Executive

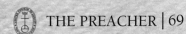

Somebody's Calling My Name

In 1961, four years after they arrived in New York City to work for the National Council of Churches, Andrew and Jean Young sat in their Queens living room and turned on the television.

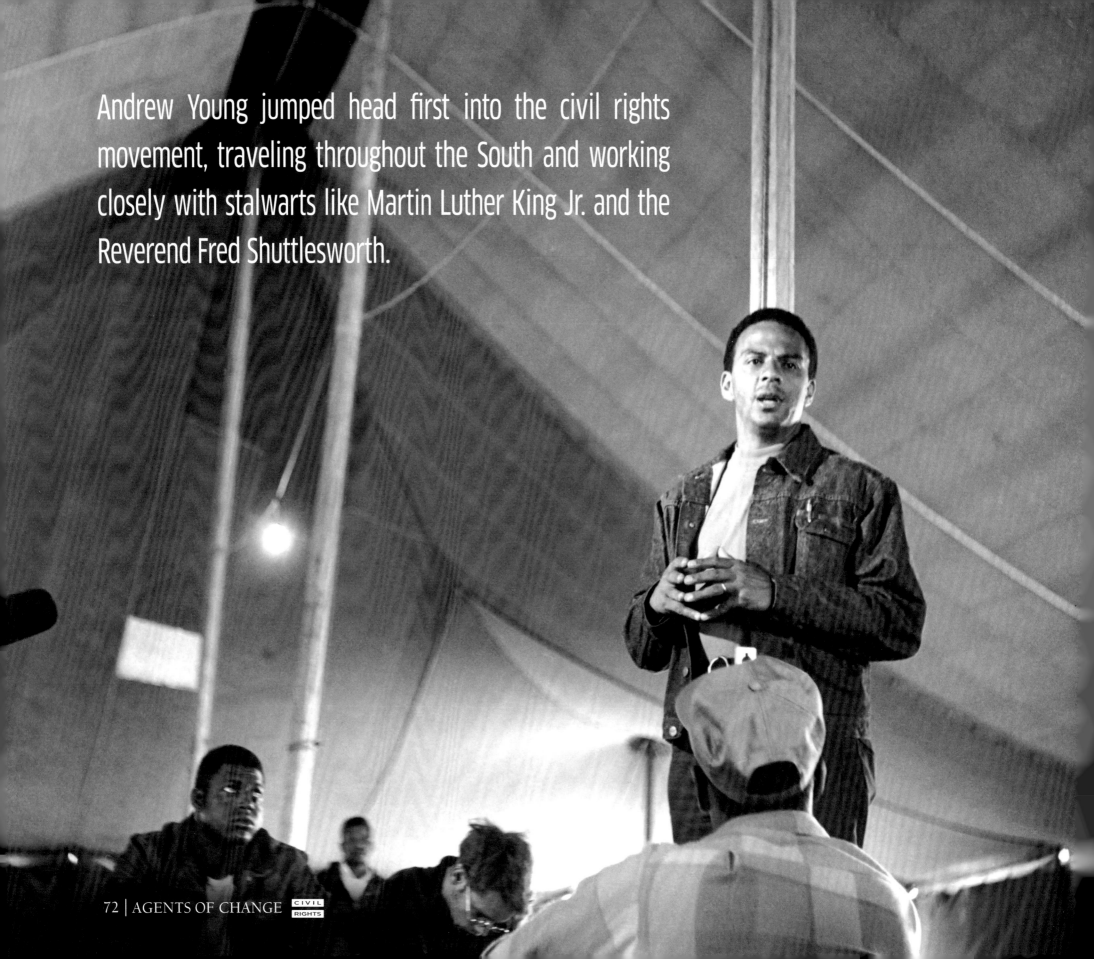

Andrew Young jumped head first into the civil rights movement, traveling throughout the South and working closely with stalwarts like Martin Luther King Jr. and the Reverend Fred Shuttlesworth.

On NBC News, they watched young people in Nashville, including John Lewis, Diane Nash, C. T. Vivian, and Bernard Lafayette, fight for and get arrested for the cause of civil rights.

The movement was catching fire in the South. By the end of the telecast, the Youngs had decided it was time to go back South. "I've had about enough of 'church work' and am anxious to do the work of the church," Young wrote at the time.

He soon found himself in Atlanta working in voter education for the Citizenship School Program housed at the Southern Christian Leadership Conference headed by Martin Luther King Jr. Young had met King in 1957 when both were invited by their fraternity, Alpha Phi Alpha, to speak at Talladega College. Young often joked that he was only invited to be there in case King didn't show up.

At the SCLC, Young answered mail, wrote letters, and did research for King's speeches. But within a year Young was working closely with the senior staff and quickly joined the inner circle as one of King's top strategic lieutenants. From that point on, as a trusted aide Young played a key role in every major decision that helped the SCLC shape the civil rights movement. In 1964, he went with the delegation to Oslo, Norway, where King accepted the Nobel Peace Prize.

That same year, Young was named executive director of the SCLC, where he helped craft strategy that led to the passage of the Civil Rights Act of 1964 and the Voting Rights Act of 1965. He was heavily involved in major movement campaigns in hotspots like Selma, Birmingham, Albany, St. Augustine, and all of Mississippi.

In 1968, he was on the balcony in Memphis.

BIRMINGHAM 1963

Left: Birmingham Fire Department aims fire hoses directly at protesters, 1963.

Middle: The Sixteenth Street Baptist Church bombing killed four innocent girls, in one of the most tragic events of the civil rights movement on September 15, 1963.

Right Middle: Police confronting protesters.

Bottom Left: Police dog attacks protesters May 1963.

Right: President Lyndon B. Johnson signs into law the Civil Rights Act of 1964.

Next page: March on Washington 1963. Years later, Young brought his wife, Jean, and their daughters, Lisa, Paula, and Andrea back to the Washington Mall.

An Appeal to You from

MATHEW AHMANN	ISAIAH MINKOFF
EUGENE CARSON BLAKE	A. PHILIP RANDOLPH
JAMES FARMER	WALTER REUTHER
MARTIN LUTHER KING, JR.	ROY WILKINS
JOHN LEWIS	WHITNEY YOUNG

to MARCH on
WASHINGTO
WEDNESDAY AUGUST 28, 19

America faces a crisis . . .
Millions of Negroes are denied freedom . . .
Millions of citizens, black and white, are unemploy

We demand: — Meaningful Civil Rights
— Full and Fair Employme
— Massive Federal Works
— Decent Housing
— The Right to Vote
— Adequate Integrated Ed

In your community, groups are mobilizing for the March
get information on how to go to Washington by calling c
organizations, religious organizations, trade unions, fra
ganizations and youth groups.

National Office —

MARCH ON WASHING
FOR JOBS AND FREE

New York 27

Top Left: Andrew Young consoles injured protesters, St. Augustine, Florida, 1964.

Top Right: St. Augustine Beach, Reverend C. T. Vivian confronts racial discrimination with a "Wade In."

Left Middle: Black children integrate the swimming pool of the Monson Motor Lodge. To force them out, the owner pours acid into the water.

Bottom: Police confronting protesters.

Bottom Left: Police assault beach goers as they try to integrate the beach.

Bottom Right: Andrew Young meets Martin Luther King Jr. for the first time in 1957.

 # We were living in Queens, New York,
and we just bought a house.

JOHN LEWIS came on television with a Nashville sit-in story. And we were sitting there looking at these young people. I had actually been down to Nashville and met with them, and I was working with them somewhat, but to see them in their national perspective on national television, Jean said, it's time for us to go back home. I said, we are home—we just bought this house. She said, "New York will never be my home. I said your home, anywhere south of Atlanta." And she was determined. She reminded me I had said we would live in New York for four to six years and it had been four years.

I had just gotten a letter from Martin Luther King. And one of his assistants in New York had come to have dinner with us and talk with me about coming back to the South. It was complicated, but I ended up quitting my job, selling our house, and accepting a job with the Southern Christian Leadership Conference. But I had to do it through the United Church of Christ because they had tax exempt status and could receive grants as contributions.

So I received a grant for a citizenship education project where we trained people to read and write to register to vote and to teach their neighbors to register to vote and pass the literacy test. We understood, always, that the hope of the South was voter registration. We actually trained six hundred or more grassroots leaders. To show how significant it was, two in our first group were the parents of the House Majority Whip in Congress. We almost laid the foundation in the 1960s for what we see now, for sixty years later James Clyburn is now the majority whip leader of the Congress of the United States.

MARTIN

I had met Martin in 1957 at Talladega College. The fraternity that we both belong to had a religious emphasis week. I always said that he was the famous one and they invited him, but then they got to thinking he might not be able to come so they invited me as a backup. We both showed up and that's the first time I met him for any length of time. We were on a program together most of the day. And in the course of that time, we realized that Jean and his wife Coretta had grown up in the same little Alabama town and had gone to the same high school.

Martin suggested we stop off in Montgomery while driving back to Thomasville and meet his new baby. We both had new baby girls. We never talked about politics. We never talked about civil rights. He was just fascinated with his baby girl. And I was fascinated with my baby girl. So, we were just playing dads. But it established a relationship that opened the door for me to come back to the South, to work with him.

Finally, in 1961, we left the National Council of Churches and came back to Atlanta. I ended up in an office just across the hall from Martin and Dora McDonald, his secretary. We didn't yet have a place to stay in Atlanta. Jean went to stay with her mother in Marion while I was looking for a house. Dora McDonald asked if I would help answer Dr. King's mail. I said I'd be honored to. She gave me an egg crate full of mail. One of the things that Martin had had trouble keeping up with was the letters from his fans and friends.

So that ended up becoming my job. I'd write the replies out longhand, Dora would type them, and Martin would sign them. He got the idea that this was working pretty well, but he didn't realize that I was the one answering and wondered how I knew so much about what he was thinking about. Dora told him, well, he went through the same schools you did and he kind of studied you. But it really did force me to read everything Martin wrote. And also to try to think like he was thinking about the world in which we lived. That turned out to be quite helpful in the future because I ended up being his executive vice president. But it meant I had to do what he should do.

ANDREW YOUNG ATTACKED AND

BEATEN BY THE KLAN as he leads a march through St. Augustine, Florida, June 9, 1964.

1964 NOBEL PEACE PRIZE

Who Goes

SCLC Expense {
Dr + Mrs. King, Yoki + Marty
Dr + Mrs Abernathy
Bernard Lee · Dora McDonald
Andrew Young
Bayard Rustin } special Assistance
Wyatt Walker

Self-paying members of Party {
Dr + Mrs M.L. King, Sr.
Harry + Lucy Wachtel (Local Counsel)
Dr + Mrs Arthur Logan
Mrs Dorothy Cotton
Lillie Hunter
Carol Hoover
Rev. Logan Kearse
Rev. Richard Bartles
Rev. O.M. Hoover
Noel Mardon, Rita McClain

Protocol

Care for King Children
Fares for family
Letter to Committee
whom to address, order
Time requirement   how many Amer. can
in Oslo, Stockholm   attend official funct.
how many official functions
what type
arrangement
Fauntroy + Norwegian Amb.

Top: Dr. Martin Luther King Jr. was presented the Nobel Peace Prize on December 10, 1964, in Oslo, Norway.

Above: Dr. Martin Luther King Jr. at the celebration of his 1964 Nobel Peace Prize with Rabbi Jacob Rothschild, Atlanta, Georgia.

Middle: Dr. Martin Luther King Jr. and Coretta Scott King proceed through the streets of Oslo.

Left: Andrew Young's notebook that he used to organize the trip.

Top Left: Nobel Peace Prize Delegation, December 1964.

Middle page: Nobel Peace Prize Medallion.

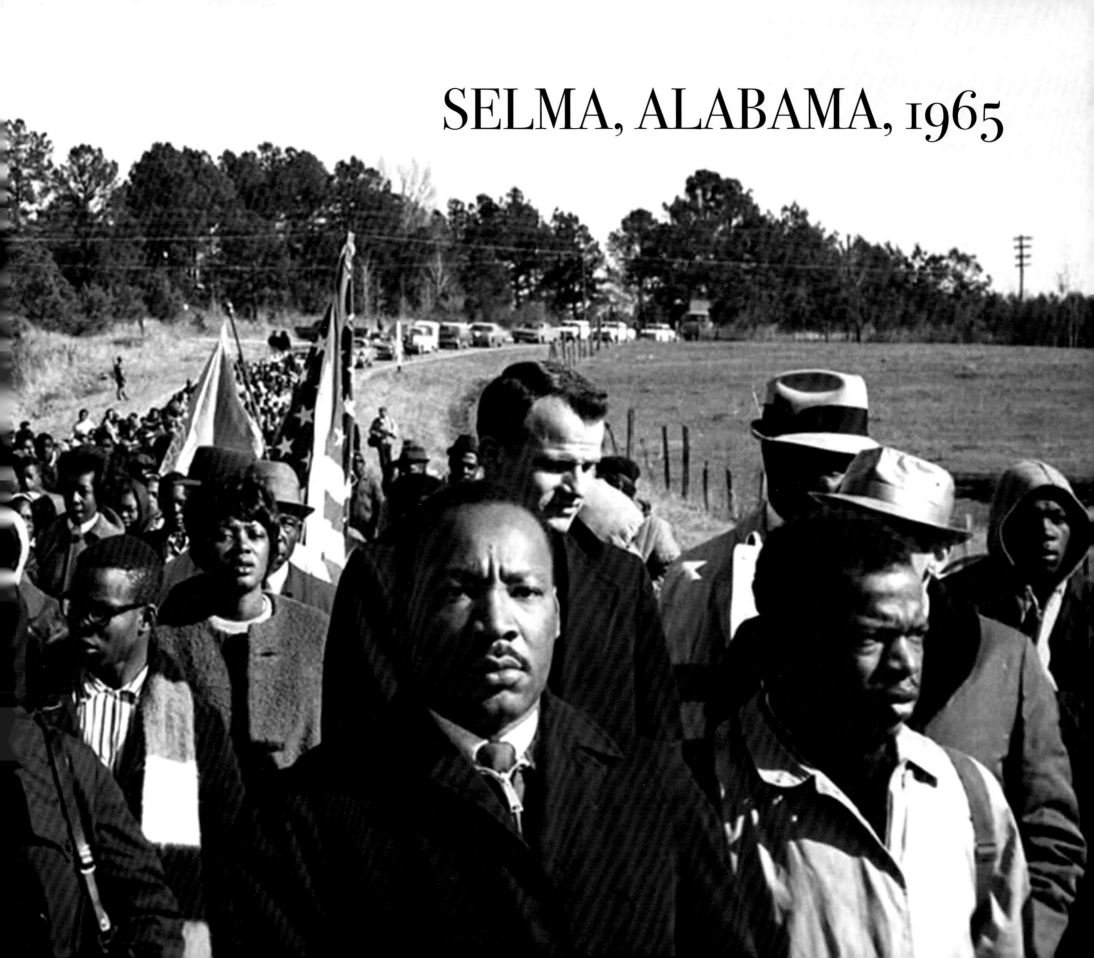

SELMA, ALABAMA, 1965

Left: On "Bloody Sunday," Alabama State Troopers confront protesters led by John Lewis and Hosea Williams, March 7, 1965.

Above: Amelia Boynton lies on ground after being clubbed unconscious during the attack.

Bottom Left: Young listens as injunction is read to block continuation of the march.

Right Top: King and Young at Montgomery Airport.

Right Top: President Johnson signs the Voting Rights Act August 6, 1965.

Right Bottom: Marchers on the 54-mile trek to Montgomery on March 23, 1965; front row, Bernard Lafayette, Andrew Young, and James Orange. John Lewis is over Young's right shoulder.

Left: Will Henry "Do-Right" Rogers marches down Robert Gardner Farm Road in Lowndes County on March 23, 1965.

Below: Andrew Young taking a break during the march.

Right: Andrew Young braving the cold temperature, Selma, Alabama, 1965.

MEMPHIS

When he was in New York on the way to the Poor People's Campaign. **I remember him saying, you know, we have to be clinically insane to think that a crazy bunch of young folk like you all,** and he was talking about himself too, would be able to change this world and redeem the soul of America.

KING PLANTS A SEED

He said, we probably won't live to forty, but if we live past forty, we should realize that we're going to have to make it to at least one hundred, because it is gonna take at least that long to get the South straightened out. We were pretty much right on target.

MEMPHIS

The night before he went to Memphis—I didn't know he was going—we had a meeting with Harry Belafonte, Gary, Indiana Mayor Dick Hatcher, and John Conyers, the Congressman from Detroit. They were talking about how the real challenge was to get the energy and vitality of the civil rights movement into politics. When we got through, it was about midnight and I said, you know, we don't have to be in Washington until about six tomorrow. So why don't you just sleep in and I'll wake you up around three o'clock when we can get the five o'clock shuttle. He said no, I'm going to take a six o'clock flight in the morning to Memphis. I said, but you just got back. He said, yeah, but I promised them I'd come and lead another march.

I said, well, you really shouldn't go back by yourself with just you and Ralph and Bernard Lee. We need some staff there with you when we have a big march. He said no, the sanitation workers are pretty good organizers, we will have a good march and I'll catch the afternoon plane. And I'll be back here by six o'clock.

Well, it didn't work that way. The last thing that we talked about before he went to Memphis was a switch to politics . . . I'd rather not talk about his death because it was a complete shock. We were totally unprepared for it. Everything we had planned was geared toward Washington, to demonstrate how to help the needs of the poor. We never really got there.

Left: National Guard in Memphis, Tennessee, 1968.

Right Bottom: Andrew Young consulting Dr. King and Rabbi Herschel, Memphis, 1968.

ON KING'S DEATH

A few days before, we were in New York. Martin was in a kind of mellow mood and he said, you know, we have to be clinically insane to think that this bunch of rabble-rousers can save this nation in one lifetime. He said, we might not live to forty, but if we do it's going to be a struggle till at least age one hundred. Because nobody knows how deep the sickness is that we have to deal with."

I was not sad when he was killed. I was envious. I felt like, why not me? Let me go to heaven. Why do you want to leave me in hell? Martin started with this movement at twenty-five and he had very few days off until he was shot at thirty-nine. Even now I don't believe that he's dead. I was watching this woman on the news complaining about the Roe v. Wade decision coming up before the Supreme Court. She quoted Dr. King, saying, "the moral arc of the universe is long, but it bends toward justice." Well, it's been almost sixty years since he died and more than sixty years since he said that. And yet, he is still motivating social change on the most important issues of the day. So death is not an end. I just want to get as much done as we can in the same tradition.

Left: Memphis sanitation workers prepare to protest in March, 1968.

Right Top: T. Y. Rodgers, James Bevel, James Orange, Andrew Young, C. K. Steele, and Ben Hooks at planning meeting April 4, 1968, in Room 306 of Lorraine Hotel, Memphis, Tennessee.

Right Middle: Moments after Martin Luther King Jr. was shot on the balcony of the Lorraine Motel in Memphis, Andrew Young, Ralph David Abernathy, and a witness point to where the gunshot came from.

DR. MARTIN LUTHER KING JR.   IS ASSASSINATED AT 6:01 PM

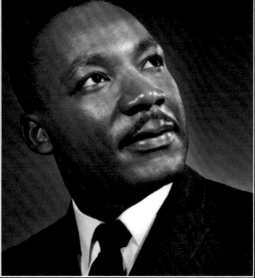

Top: Andrew Young and James Orange help load Dr. King's casket onto the airplane that will take his body home to Atlanta.

Above: On April 8, 1968, Coretta Scott King traveled to Memphis to complete the march that her husband started for the sanitation workers. *Left to Right*: Yolanda King *(daughter 13)*, Martin King III, *(son 10)* Dexter King *(son 7)* Coretta Scott King Rev. Ralph Abernathy, Andrew Young, and Rabbi Abraham Heschel.

Bottom: Funeral at Morehouse College for Martin Luther King Jr., April 9, 1968 *(left to right)* Rev. Ralph David Abernathy, Dr. Benjamin Mays, Rev. Andrew Young, and others singing.

Right Page: Funeral procession down Auburn Avenue on April 9, 1968, in Atlanta.

9 June 68

Sidney Poitier
wants that AJY.
meet each VIP
coming ~~from~~ to
Resurrection City – their
personal arrangements
are being made by
Mrs Marjorie Parker
RA3-2206

...S OF THE WEEK

...paper columnist, on what the intellec-
...king these days: *"The articulate Ne-
...rd enough, also enunciated a final sen-
...e to have all the barriers between us
...but then I would like to take my time
..."*

...ster of the late Malcolm X, on possible
..."*If you think they're going to be on
...r, you are mistaken. Newark, Detroit,
...re done by kids—frustrated children.
...re and he can take New York in two
...estimate the black man. You trained
...in your wars."*

...sident of National Educational Tele-
...blic television's responsibility is: *"It
...se issues that have inflamed our na-
...tting laziness and indifference con-
...that makes possible the murders of
...the Martin Luther Kings, the thou-
...around this world."*

...**artin Poussaint**, professor of psychiatry at Tufts
University in Boston, on black leaders: *"Negro leaders
have often found it difficult to get other black people to
follow them. These people have seen white success and
black failure all their lives and thus question the skills as well as the motives of the
person trying to lead them."*

Sidney Poitier, on why he is at Resurrection
City: *"I came down here not as a celebrity but as someone who needs to estab-
lish roots among people who gave me
birth. If blacks and whites cannot work
together the nation cannot survive."*

Poitier

30

- S.C.L.C. quit Resurrection City
  - Abandoned ~~too~~ without a fight
  - P.R. dis-advantage

- Enhanced with Gimmick of Resurrection City
  becomes end
- Solidarity Day should have been called off

- We conditioned people WRONG
  publicity Gimmicks + not militant action

- Arrived with support and declined
- Embassy not sufficient – an intellectual concept.

- defensive on violence
  - must trust people
  - only way you can lose is to
    think about behavior
  - can't play their Game

STATEMENT BY DR. MARTIN LUTHER KING JR., PRESIDENT
Southern Christian Leadership Conference
Atlanta, Georgia
December 4, 1967

LADIES & GENTLEMEN:

Last week the staff of the Southern Christian Leadership Conference held one of the mo...

important meetings we have ever convened. We had intensive discussions and analyses of our

work and of the challenges which confront us and our nation, and at the end we made a decisio...

which I wish to announce today.

The Southern Christian Leadership Conference will lead waves of the nation's poor an...

disinherited to Washington, D.C., next spring to demand...

United States government and to secure at least...

We will go there, we will demand to be h...

If this means forcible repression of our moveme...

before. If this means scorn or ridicule, we emb...

receive. If it means jail, we accept it willingly,...

by exploitation and discrimination. But we hope,...

Washington will receive at first a sympathetic un...

matic expansion of non-violent demonstrations in...

In short, we will be petitioning our government f...

militant non-violent actions until that government...

We now have begun preparations for the W...

taking new assignments to organize people to go t...

areas. This will be no mere one-day march in W...

by suffering and outraged citizens who will go to s...

taken to provide jobs and income for the poor.

POOR PEOPLE'S NEWS

WASHINGTON D.C...

SOUTHERN CHRISTIAN LEA...
Bernard Lafayette, Campaign...

334 Auburn Ave. N.E.
Atlanta Georgia, 30303
(404)-522-1420

1401 U St. N.W.
Washington D.C.
(202)-462-7000

FOR RELEASE: March 15, 196...

Black and White Toge...

AMERICAN INDIANS, POOR WHI...

JOIN POOR PEOPLE'...

ATLANTA, GA., March 15-- A historic...

group leaders ended here today with a declar...

Poor People's Campaign in Washington, D....

Representatives of American Indians, P...

Americans and Negroes, meeting here at th...

Leadership Conference (SCLC), said their...

and participate in the Campaign which was...

The minority group leaders selected e...

Doctor Martin Luther King and Doctor Ra...

leaders on the National Poor People's Ste...

Doctor King, SCLC President, expre...

meeting and said: "This is a highly signi...

co-operation, understanding, and a dete...

"YOU CAN'T KEEP US DOWN"
THE WORLD KNOWS THAT WE BLACK FOLK
ARE SURELY FREEDOM BOUND...
WE ARE REACHING FOR THE CLOUDS...
YOU CAN'T KEEP US DOWN...
PUSH US BACK STILL WE SHALL RISE...
IN SEARCH OF FREEDOM'S CROWN...
FAITH HAS WILLED FOR US BLACK MEN...
YOU CAN'T KEEP US DOWN...
THO YOU PUT US IN JAIL...
YOU KNOW YOU WILL FAIL...
TO MAKE US GIVE IN...
WE WILL WALK THE PICKET LINE...
BRING FREEDOM TO OUR TOWN...
YOU SHOULD KNOWN JIM CROW IS DEAD...
SO YOU CAN'T KEEP US DOWN...
(ERNEST REED)   J. EDWARD HAYCRAFT

"In Resurrection CITY"

Left corner: Message for SCLC
Left corner middle: Jet Magazine 1968
Bottom Left: Andy's note pad.
Middle: SCLC Press release
Top middle: Resurrection City, June 1968
Washington D.C.

REFLECTING POOL

CAMPAIGN

RENCE Martin Luther King Jr., President
ea Williams, Campaign Field Director

68-R-16

SH-AMERICANS

ON CAMPAIGN

american minority

mous support for the

g.

poor whites, Mexican-

the Southern Christian

husiastically support

CLC.

t the session to join

y of SCLC and other

ee.

s to delegates at the

e beginning of a new

or people of all colors

t life and respect for

Left: Statement from Dr. King moving forward with the initiative for the Poor People Campaign   **Above:** Map of Resurrection City where the poor of the nation would gather.

Left: Andrew Young securing mules for the Poor People's Campaign in Marks, Mississippi, 1968.

Middle: SCLC drumming up support for the Poor People's Campaign.

Right Left: Andrew Young and Joan Baez and group of SCLC field workers singing.

POOR PEOPLE'S CAMPAIGN 1968

SCLC

POOR PEOPLE'S CAMPAIGN 1968

Atlanta's Welcoming To The Poor Peoples March

Outstanding International Talent

Speakers — Mrs. Martin Luther King, Jr.
Father Groppi

POOR PEOPLE'S CAMPAIGN 1968

Atlanta's Welcoming To The Poor Peoples March

Outstanding International Talent

Speakers — Mrs. Martin Luther King, Jr.
Father Groppi

THURSDAY, MAY 9, 1968

Program Begins 8:30

ATLANTA CIVIC CENTER

Advance Donation — — — — $2.00

We Participated In His March, Now Let's Participate In His Dream

542

Southern Christian Leadership Conference
Poor Peoples Campaign-1968

FUND RAISING FOR THE POOR PEOPLES CAMPAIGN

A Quaker Action Group
20 South 12th Street
Philadelphia, Pa. 19107
LO7-3150

Why Money
Money is needed to support the 3000 poor people who are going to Washington to demonstrate for Jobs and Income. They are poor—that's why they are demonstrating—and they cannot support themselves. Many of the participants have been threatened with economic reprisals if they demonstrate for their rights.

Organizing a campaign of this sort is expensive. Printing, mailings, and offices all cost money. SCLC and Dr. King do not receive grants from the governments. The money must come from concerned individuals.

Gifts in Kind
Many times it's easier to get gifts of materials rather than money. Wholesale merchants, retailers, etc. should be contacted and asked to donate non-perishable foodstuffs, shoes, clothing, and stationery supplies. Please collect only new clothing and shoes. Poor people have had enough experience with cast-off clothing.

How
1. Contact friends and neighbors, explain the campaign, the need and ask for money.
2. Contact groups, churches, Friends meetings, pro-Civil Rights labor unions, Civil Rights groups and business-men. Explain the campaign, the need and ask for money.
3. Ask groups you are in contact with to send out a fund appeal to those on their mailing lists.

Where to send money
1. To your local SCLC office.
2. To SCLC, Poor Peoples Campaign
   334 Auburn Ave., NE, Atlanta, Ga., 30303

Where to send gifts in kind
1. Take the materials to your local SCLC office.
2. Write Washington SCLC, 1401 "U" St., NW, Washington, D.C. Tell SCLC what you have collected and they will notify you when it is needed.

POOR PEOPLE'S CAMPAIGN

DISBURSEMENTS

Gladys McFadden Singers (5/16/68 Rally)	$ 600.00
SCLC March Staff (Expense Money 5/17/68)	100.00
Larry Huff (Miscellaneous 5/20/68)	625.00

TRANSPORT:

5/16	Greyhound	$7,002.83
5/17	Greyhound	356.70
5/20	Traveler's Aid	68.80
5/20	"	170.40
5/21	PAT	456.40
5/23	PAT	111.00
5/23	Bob Connen (Gasoline)	3.00
5/23	Humble Oil Co.	8.96
5/25	Traveler's Aid	74.50
5/25	Herbert Bean	17.55
5/31	Traveler's Aid	45.80
6/12	Traveler's Aid	32.40
6/14	Marcher to Wash. D.C. Court	19.70
6/14	N.W. Airlines (Staff)	71.40
6/14	N.W. Airlines (Staff)	78.10
		8,507.54

FOOD FOR MARCHERS:

5/17	Kroger Grocery Co.	45.33
5/23	Sixth Mt. Zion Bapt. Church (Food & Svs.)	334.00
6/6	Washington D.C.	8.81
6/3	Pittsburgh Hilton	22.00
		410.14

PRINTING, PUBLICITY & POSTAGE:

5/20	S & S Printing Co.	206.17
5/20	"	98.58
5/23	Sign Service, Inc.	50.00
5/23	North Side Christian Ministry	55.00
5/23	Stationery & Postage	50.00
6/6	Service Department Printing	80.00
6/6	Western Union	39.69
6/6	P.O. Naly Co. (Stickers(	1.90
6/13	S & S Printing Co.	108.12
6/14	Central Baptist Church	28.98
6/14	ADA (Postage)	180.00
		899.44

SUPPLIES:

5/23	Matthew Moore (Refund)	5.00
5/23	Agnes Green (Refund)	25.00
5/31	K Mart (Marcher's Clothing)	94.74
6/6	Marshall's Sweaters	112.50
6/6	Sunny's Surplus Clothing (Wash. D.C.)	76.20
		313.44

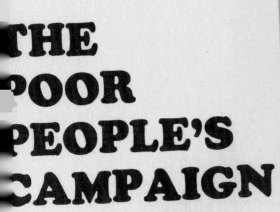

THE
POOR
PEOPLE'S
CAMPAIGN

ROBERT FRANCIS KENNEDY   IS ASSASSINATED AT 12:15 AM

LOS ANGELES, CALIFORNIA   JUNE 6, 1968

say that I feel in my own heart the same kind of feeling. I had a member of my family killed, but he was killed by a white man. But we have to make an effort in the United States, we have to make an effort to understand, to go beyond these rather difficult times . . ."

Excerpt of Senator Robert F. Kennedy speech
Indianapolis, Indiana
Evening of April 4, 1968

JUNE 8, 1968 *Funeral of Robert F. Kennedy*

Left to Right: (*Back row*) Jacqueline Kennedy, Rev. Ralph David Abernathy, Rev. Andrew Young, and (*Front row*) Ethel Kennedy (*widow*)

Left: Giving mule rides to children in Atlanta during the Poor People's March.

Middle: Andrew Young and Cesar Chavez.

Inset: Anniversary death of Dr. King, *(from left)* Christine King Farris, Angela Farris, Alberta King *(Dr. King's mother)*, Cesar Chavez, Bernice A. King *(daughter)*, Coretta Scott King *(Dr. King's wife)*, Andrew Young, Yolanda King *(daughter)*, Martin Luther King III *(son)*, and Dexter Scott King *(son)*.

Right: Leading the Poor People's March, from right, Andrew Young, Juanita Abernathy, Cesar Chavez, and A. D. King.

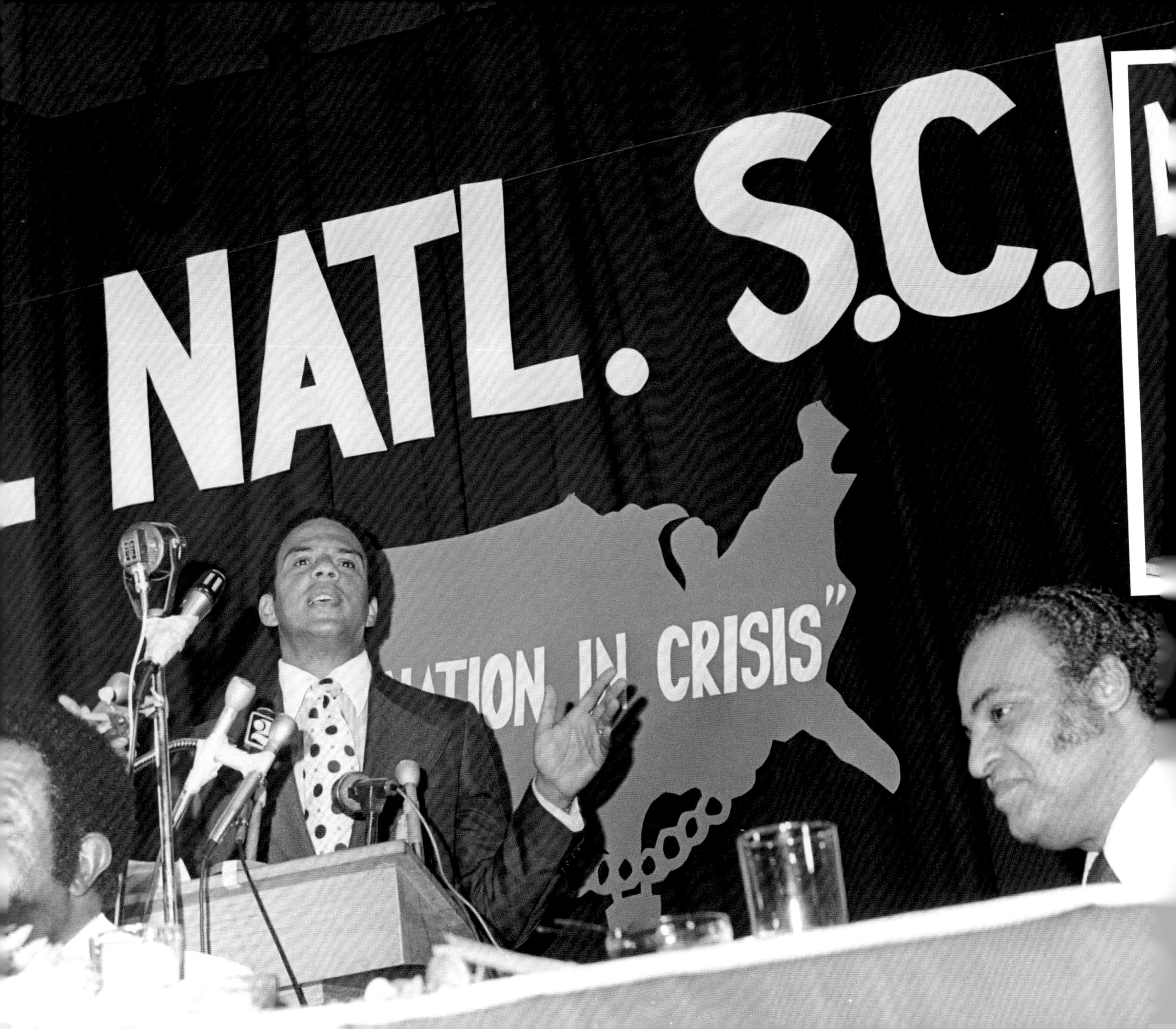
NATL. S.C.
IN CRISIS"

MOVING the CIVIL RIGHTS
movement to politics

It was what I thought it would be. As far back as my involvement in SCLC, usually when Dr. King would go to see President Johnson, I was with him. I realized that everything we were marching for in the streets had to be translated by the Congress and the president into law for it to be meaningful.

Left: Andrew Young speaking at SCLC Convention.

Top: Andrew Young presents the Reverend Ralph David Abernathy with an award, while the Reverend Joseph Lowery looks on.

Bottom Right: Andrew Young and NAACP President Ben Hooks.

CONGRESS

Young
for Congress

THINK
YOUNG
Andrew Young
for Congress.

I Guess I'm Running for Congress

WHEN YOUNG WAS ELECTED IN GEORGIA TO SERVE IN THE UNITED STATES HOUSE OF REPRESENTATIVES, HE BROUGHT CIVIL RIGHTS AND MARTIN LUTHER KING JR. WITH HIM TO WASHINGTON.

Toward the end of his life, King had begun to talk about how the movement could shift its strategies from protesting in the streets to being in a position to make laws and create legislation.

That meant getting elected willing, capable people with courage and good priorities. Young wasn't particularly interested in seeking public office, but pressure from within the movement prodded him to run. He lost his first race in 1970 but was elected to Congress in 1972 representing parts of metro Atlanta. He won 95 percent of the black vote and 23 percent of the white vote, becoming the first black Representative from Georgia since Jefferson Long in 1871, during Reconstruction. Along with Barbara Jordan of Texas, who was also elected for the first time in 1972, Young was among the few Blacks in Congress. He used his experience as an activist to become a pragmatic and grassroots politician, eager to learn and negotiate.

"I consider this victory a little more than just being the first Black man to go to Congress from this Deep South state," Young said at the time. "I see this as a city-wide mandate of people of both races working together to achieve the kind of representation that this area so badly needs."

Young served on the House Committee on Banking and Currency and the subcommittee on Housing, Transportation, and Finance. He sponsored legislation that established a U.S. Institute for Peace, the African Development Bank, and the Chattahoochee River National Park. He was also an early proponent of the Urban Mass Transportation Assistance Act that facilitated the building of mass transit systems like Atlanta's MARTA. Young argued that while cities like Atlanta would see an overall benefit in mass public transportation, inner-city black and white poor people who didn't own cars would especially benefit from the $1 billion in federal support.

It was in Congress that Young developed his interest in foreign policy, a path that would soon lead him to Asia, Latin America, and Africa.

THINK YOUNG
Andrew Young for Congress.

AN DY NEEDS YOUR HELP

SIGN UP TODAY TO:
1 CANVASS By Phone or foot
2 Work all day Nov 3 to get out the vote
3 Work morning table at Ga. State
4 Work at the Northside Office

GSU Students for Andrew Young

THINK YOUNG
Andrew Young for Congress.

Left: Campaign workers ready for the day's tasks.

Top Right: Andrew Young contemplating next move.

Bottom Right: Campaign worker excited about the campaign pins.

Middle Right: Jean Young and her family.

KODAK TRI X PAN FILM

THINK YOUNG
Andrew Young for Congress

→17A   →18   →18A   →19   →19A

Young campaigning all over the city of Atlanta.

KODAK SAFETY FILM

→ 20A → 21

Young for Congress

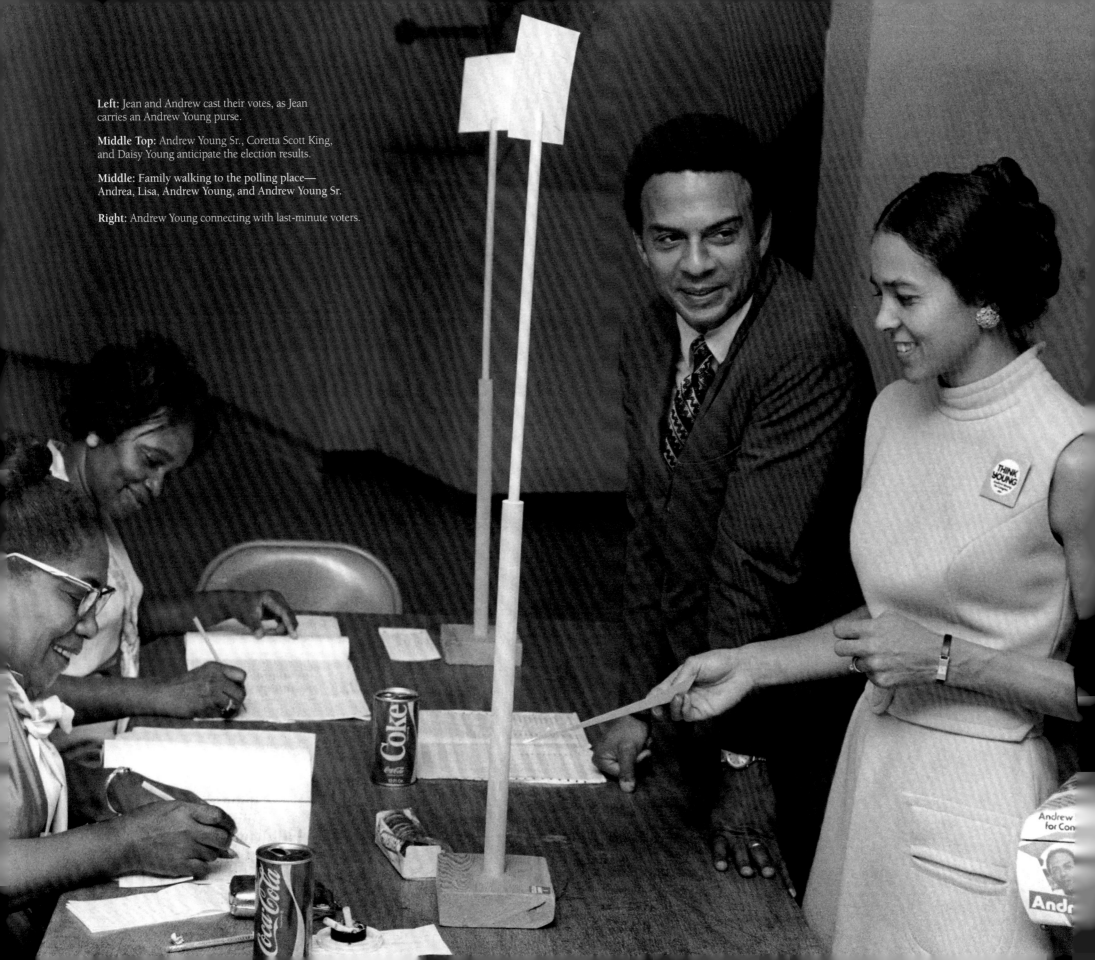

Left: Jean and Andrew cast their votes, as Jean carries an Andrew Young purse.

Middle Top: Andrew Young Sr., Coretta Scott King, and Daisy Young anticipate the election results.

Middle: Family walking to the polling place— Andrea, Lisa, Andrew Young, and Andrew Young Sr.

Right: Andrew Young connecting with last-minute voters.

I didn't want to get into politics. I always saw myself as a community organizer. And after this meeting with Harry Belafonte, I was talking with him and trying to get him to raise some money in case somebody wanted to run for Congress.

He didn't say anything. He just turned around and picked up the phone and called his wife and said, see if you can find a time when Lena Horne, Sydney Portier and Alan King are in town. We need to run a fundraiser and it's Andy's running for Congress. And I said, wait a minute. No, I'm, I'm not running for Congress. I want to get other people to run for Congress. He said, well, Julian said he doesn't want to run. Vernon. Jordan says he doesn't want to run. Nobody left but you. I said, well, I guess, I guess I'm running for Congress. And I was familiar with the problems of Reconstruction.

The district was the entire length of Fulton County all the way to the north and almost all the way to the south. It was probably only about 28% black. And I thought someone had to run for Congress. It wasn't a matter of winning or losing. It was a matter of making a move toward the Congress, toward politics to bring some of the massive energy of the 1960s into the political arena. So, I wasn't all that concerned about winning, but I was concerned about organizing and running and learning what it was. I ended up losing to Fletcher Thompson. And the interesting thing was that I had said something about one of the Black Panthers in Chicago who was machine gunned in his bed. I said that these are really bright kids. They are talking bad, but they haven't lifted a finger to hurt anyone. They shouldn't be murdered for their thoughts. Well, that made me in some people's mind, a supporter of the Black Panthers. And so, my opponent put out a picture of me that came from Mississippi. The Klan had thrown children on their way to kindergarten and first grade and threw them plate glass windows. They were really roughing up little kids. So, we went back there and walked the kids to school. Martin Luther King, Joan Baez and Hosea Williams. I was talking to the kid because he was one of those that had been roughed up. I was telling him not to be afraid, look away or hide his face. I told him to remember what he did to you and let him know that he didn't stop you from wanting to go to school. So, I was trying to pump this kid up, to get on his mean face. I don't think I was looking mean, but I hadn't shaved in a couple of days. So, my opponent cut the little boy out and made a picture of me. I don't know how many hundreds of thousands they made, they printed, but they were all over town and the signs, it was a picture of me saying "If Andrew Young is elected, the black Panthers are going to get your daughter."

That was the kind of campaign that was being run and I lost. But I didn't in any way think of stopping. The American civil liberties union went to court, to challenge the redistricting. And it created a district that was about 32% black and it was mostly in the city of Atlanta, so I had a better chance. I was running against Rodney Cook and we really had a good, honest, open, friendly campaign and I managed to win.

Left: Community organizer Susie LaBord makes the case for Andrew Young.

Top Right: James Orange and Andrew Young hand out campaign information.

Right: Andrew Young checking on the progress of the campaign.

Next Page Left: Andrew Young anticipating what the day holds for the campaign.

Next Page Right: Jean Young makes the case for her husband at the Motor Hotel.

Atlanta's got Young ideas.
Send Andrew Young to Congress.
ATLANTA
AMERICANA
MOTOR HOTEL

DIPPING INTO
ATLANTA POLITICS

 **After I lost the race,** something very significant happened. Mayor Sam Massell called me and asked me if I'd be willing to serve as the co-chairman of the community relations commission for the city.

Well, my co-chair was Archbishop Thomas Donnellan of the Roman Catholic diocese. That had the effect of making me respectable. And through no part of my own, there were four or five trade union strikes in Atlanta. The Archbishop was seldom in town, so I ended up being called to these situations and because of what I'd been doing in the civil rights movement was negotiating between people who disagree violently and vociferously, I kind of was in a pretty good position to mediate. What I found out was that it was little emotional, hot buttons. At one of the plans, a woman forgot her diabetes medicine and asked to go home to get it. And her supervisor said if you go home, you lose a day's pay. So, she didn't go home. And then she passed out about lunchtime and everybody said, the rumor got out that she was dead, and everybody walked off the job. And it was, it was simply a matter of getting her some medicine, convincing people that she was not

dead and taking up the grievances, most of which evolved around insensitivity. I found that most of the plant managers and plant owners were really good people and they were shocked that these decisions that were quite often made at a much lower level without any decision, any discussion, could have all been eliminated. But I got to know and be known by people, black and white, management and labor. Every last one of these five or six strikes, we were able to resolve in two or three days. And it was simply doing what I'd been doing all my life, talking to people who differed.

I grew up in New Orleans talking to white people. So, there was nothing unusual for me talking to white people. And I went to black schools and I was black, so I understood the plight of the workers. I had been to jail and with the sanitation workers, so I had credibility on both sides.

Even after losing the 1970 congressional race, Andrew Young still had his eyes on Washington, D.C. He regrouped and quickly launched his 1972 campaign.

The Chance of a Century!

An Open Letter to the Black Community

by Dr. Benjamin E. Mays

1870

Jefferson Long — the first and only black Congressman from Georgia.

1972

Andrew Young — The chance of a century to make history November 7th.

In 1870, one hundred and two years ago, Jefferson Long, a black man, became a Congressman from Georgia. He was the first and the last.

In 1972, we have the opportunity of a century to elect Andrew Young, a black man, to Congress.

But this historic opportunity will be lost unless there is a massive turnout of black voters on November 7th. The disappointing record of several elections in recent years shows that thousands of black registered voters in Atlanta failed to vote. In some precincts, as many as three out of four black voters did not go to the polls.

Black voters have the numbers, but each must get relatives, friends and neighbors to get serious about voting on November 7th.

Jefferson Long is a proud name in black history. In Congress, he fought for the right of black people to vote and for protection of black voters from violence.

Andrew Young has played a distinguished role in the struggle of black people. He fought for the right to vote in the last decade. He helped write the Voting Rights Act of 1965 and the Civil Rights Act of 1964. He will fight to protect those

hard-won laws in Congress, and he will work for better education, jobs, health care, housing, fair taxes, and government services for the community.

Jefferson Long made history a century ago. You can make history on November 7th by electing Andrew Young to Congress — but only if you vote and get others in the black community to vote.

It is extremely urgent that we get together this one time. This is the opportunity that comes once in a lifetime — the chance of a century. If you vote, we all win with Andrew Young in Congress. If not, we all lose.

Top Right: Campaign literature from the 1970 run.

Left: Dr. Benjamin E. Mays embraces Andrew Young, while President Carter looks on in 1979.

Right: Ad placed in 1972 by Dr. Benjamin E. Mays.

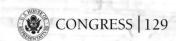

Left: Andrew and Jean Young on podium.

Top Right: Jean and Andrew at the watch party.

Right: Coretta Scott King and
Andrea Young at the watch party.

Andrew Young
for Congress

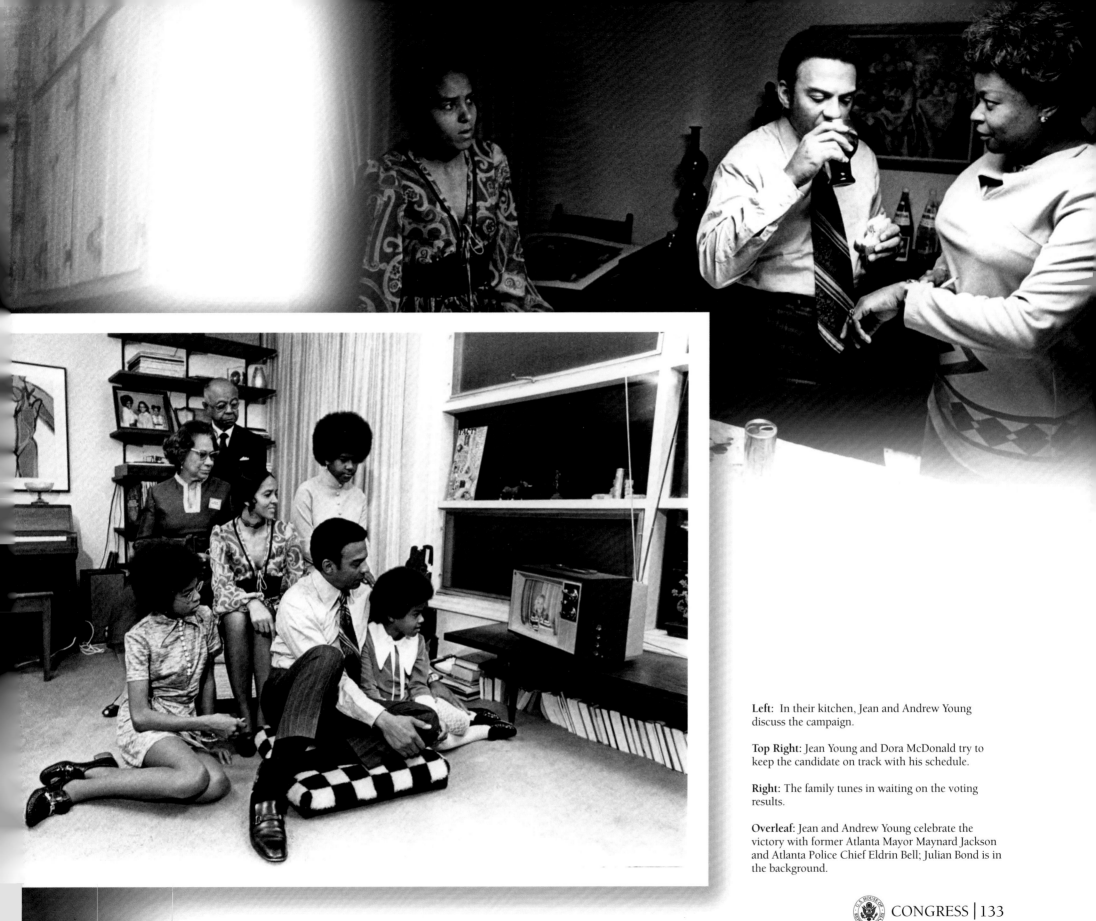

Left: In their kitchen, Jean and Andrew Young discuss the campaign.

Top Right: Jean Young and Dora McDonald try to keep the candidate on track with his schedule.

Right: The family tunes in waiting on the voting results.

Overleaf: Jean and Andrew Young celebrate the victory with former Atlanta Mayor Maynard Jackson and Atlanta Police Chief Eldrin Bell; Julian Bond is in the background.

Once I got to Congress, I was extremely well received. In fact, I was almost taken in like a celebrity and I found myself getting invited to Catherine Graham's home for dinner. That's part of the inner circle of Washington.

They treated me like I was Martin Luther King's assistance, not like I was Andrew Young, just running for Congress. I had to be very careful with the press and I was. Because of my issues with the Black Panther incident, I said very little to the press. Except that I had learned from Mayor Ivan Allen, that you have to keep a relationship with the press. He always said that he talked to the people at the Atlanta Journal-Constitution at least once or twice a month and he still couldn't get a decent story half the time. But he said that's the nature of politics and the press. Your job is to give them as much information as you can and to stay as close to them as you can. I tried to do that, in the Congress. I ended up doing a lot of the talk shows and getting a lot of national publicity. Even though I was in Congress, the national publicity was still about the civil rights movement and still is to this day.

The most significant thing that happened to me in Congress that helped me most in life, is really right up there with my relationship with Martin Luther King. was me being on the banking committee. I know nothing about banking, but banking is urban affairs and urban affairs had mass transit and I wanted to be on the mass transit subcommittee.

I was on the international finance subcommittee. And the very first meeting I went to, George Schultz, Paul VOCA, and the head of the federal reserve were all there speaking on ending the Bretton Woods agreements, and nobody asked any questions. I had never had a course in economics. I didn't know anything about the Bretton woods agreement or John Maynard Keynes. I kind of started asking around and kind of figured out a little bit about what it was about and when nobody asked any questions, they were ending the Bretton Woods agreements, which structured the economy of the world after the second world war. They were ending it so that the dollar would not be regulated by an agreement that all of the countries made together, but the dollar would be allowed to float.

Everybody was just nodding agreement because they were intimidated by these giant economists of our time. I finally raised my hand and I said, excuse me, but it seems to me that if you break up these agreements and allow the dollar to float, that people will play politics with our currency, there'll be just a kind of a free for all. And Arthur Burns, chairman of the federal reserve took a puff on his pipe and he said, "young man, you'll soon learn that the dollar does not need you to defend it."

But the fact that I raised it got the attention of George Schultz, who was the secretary of treasury. And he came up to me after the meeting and he said, 'you know, I'm constantly traveling to these international conferences and I hate to go with an all- white delegation representing the United States of America. Would you mind traveling with me sometime?

It gave me a chance to learn what's going on and he sort of took me under his wing. I flew with him to the Inter-American Development bank down in Jamaica. A few months later, I went to Kenya with him to the World Bank meeting. And we just became good friends. When I went with him to these meetings, I was flying with him on Air Force Two with all of the key financial advisors. I was really getting an education just by keeping my mouth shut and listening. I got to know heads of states.

THINK YOUNG
Andrew Young for Congress

Nigerian Foreign Minister

Panama

Above: Nigerian Foreign Minister Joseph Nanven Garba confers with Congressman Andrew Young.

Left and facing page: Andrew Young leads discussions on the development of the Panama Canal.

Senegal

NOV. 30, 1972/35¢ A JOHNSON PUBLICATION

JET

U.S. CONGRESS GETS THREE NEW BLACK LAWMAKERS

BARBARA JORDAN

YVONNE B. BURKE

THINK YOUNG
Andrew Young for Congress

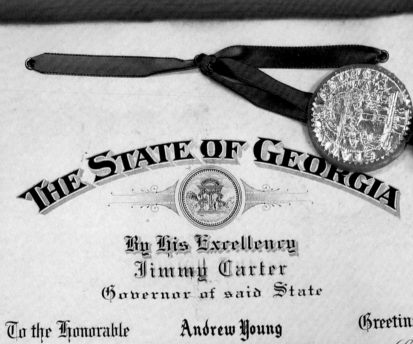

THE STATE OF GEORGIA

By His Excellency
Jimmy Carter
Governor of said State

To the Honorable   Andrew Young   Greeting:

Whereas, in conformity with the provisions of the Constitution and Laws of this State, you were on the 5th day of November Nineteen Hundred and Seventy-four elected Representative in Congress from the Fifth District of Georgia

Now, Therefore, By virtue of the power and authority in me vested by the Constitution and Laws of this State, and in pursuance of your election I do hereby commission you the said Andrew Young
Representative in Congress from the Fifth District of Georgia

This Commission shall continue in force from January 3, 1975

to January 3, 1977
and until your successor is elected and qualified, unless the same shall be vacated sooner or annulled in the manner authorized by the Constitution and Laws of this State.
Given under my hand and the Great Seal of the State at the Capitol, in the City of Atlanta, the 16th day of December in the year of our Lord One Thousand Nine Hundred and Seventy-four.

By the Governor:

Ben W. Fortson Jr.
SECRETARY OF STATE

Jimmy Carter
GOVERNOR

Left: Andrew Young on the cover of *Jet* magazine in 1972.

Left Middle: Formal certificate given to Young's mother by then-Georgia Governor Jimmy Carter.

Right: In 1972, Congressman Young, (light colored jacket) and the Congressional Black Caucus, met with Vice President Gerald Ford. The meeting was attended by, among others, Charles Rangel, Shirley Chisholm, Robert Nix, Cardiss Colins, Parren Mitchell, Gus Hawkins, Walter Fauntroy, Ralph Metcalfe, Ronald Dellums, Louis Stokes, Charles Diggs, Bill Clay and John Conyers.

Bottom Right: Congressional Black Caucus 1972.

Above: Congressman Young at a hearing.

Left: Congressman Young *(center)* hosted Atlanta Mayor Maynard Jackson *(fourth from left)* and the Reverend Joseph Lowery *(fourth from right)* at the Capitol.

Right Page: Then-Senator Joe Biden and Congressman Young at a fundraiser on May 13, 1975.

Top Left: Andrew Young rowing down the Chattahoochee River.

Left Middle: Congressmen John Frederick Seiberling and Andrew Young with former Georgia Governor George Busbee.

Bottom Left: Congressman Young and his aide running to make a vote.

Right page: Congressman Young, his son Bo, and UN Secretary Kurt Waldheim, with Senator Ted Kennedy at right.

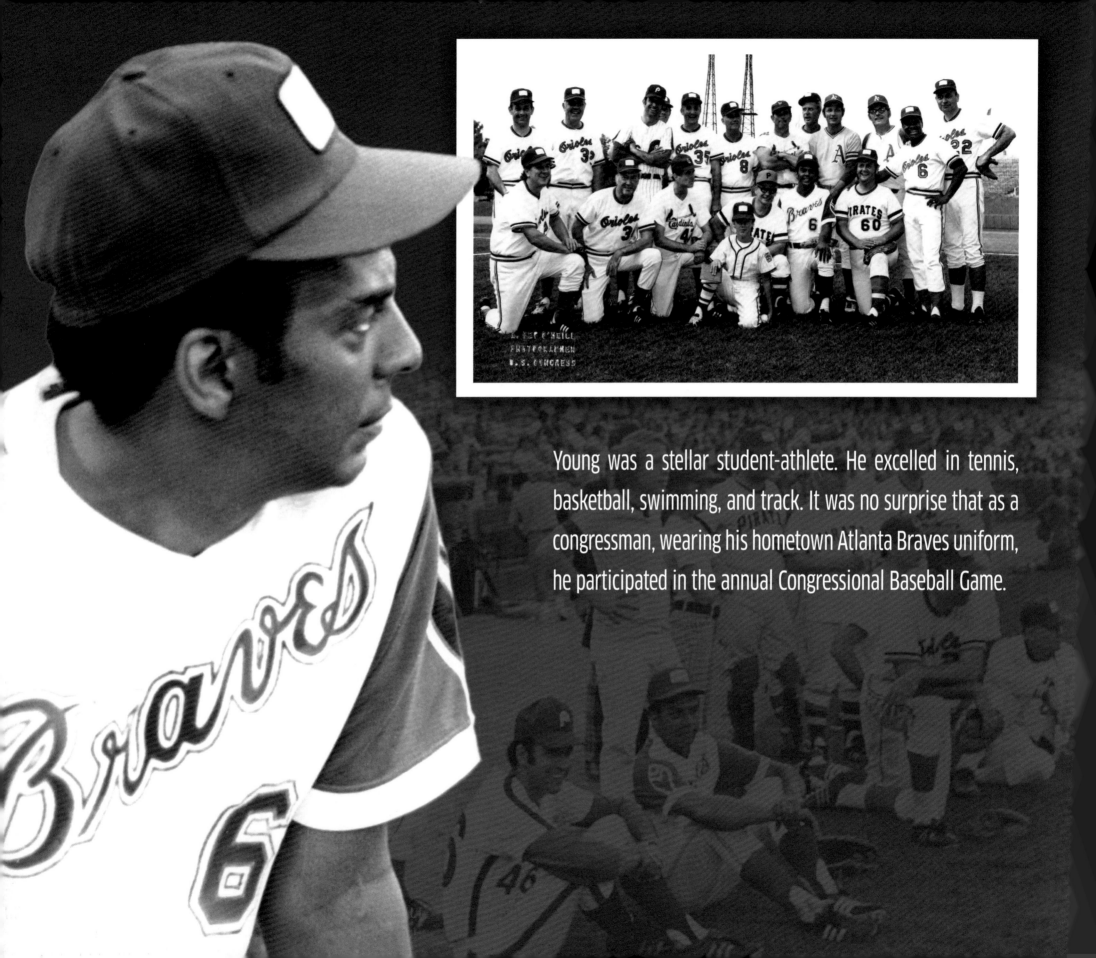

Young was a stellar student-athlete. He excelled in tennis, basketball, swimming, and track. It was no surprise that as a congressman, wearing his hometown Atlanta Braves uniform, he participated in the annual Congressional Baseball Game.

AMBASSADOR
You Couldn't

Say No to Something Like That

I N 1976, YOUNG EASILY WON HIS THIRD TERM IN THE HOUSE, SETTING UP WHAT COULD HAVE BEEN A DECADES-LONG CAREER IN CONGRESS.

But Young had been building a relationship with Georgia Governor Jimmy Carter. Young enthusiastically supported Carter's 1976 presidential bid, organizing voter registration drives, setting up meetings with members of the Congressional Black Caucus, and delivering a seconding speech at the Democratic National Convention in New York City.

After the Georgian's inauguration as president in January 1977, Young resigned from Congress and accepted Carter's nomination to become the U.S. Ambassador to the United Nations. He was the first African American to hold that position.

Young's earlier interest in foreign policy quickly became an asset, as he became the point person for the Carter Administration's foreign policy initiatives in Africa and Asia. Young effectively articulated the president's positions on human rights and liberal capitalism.

However, in 1979 reports surfaced that Young had held a private meeting with a Palestine Liberation Organization official despite earlier U.S. promises to Israel that it would not meet with the PLO until the group recognized Israel's right to exist. Young resigned the ambassadorship, and Carter would go on to lose the 1980 presidential election.

Young may strenthen UN post

By Martin F. Nolan
Globe Washington Bureau

BOSTON GLOBE 12/20

WASHINGTON — Jimmy Carter's cabinetwork is almost half completed and the cabinetmaker seems to have chosen his own sparse style: Christian competence.

The President-elect has chosen only one "outsider" so far, his Atlanta friend Bert Lance to be director of the Office of Management and Budget.

The others selected so far are familiar faces, all noncontroversial, all recipients of both bipartisan support and objective praise.

Carter, who still faces the problem of affirmative action in filling the rest of his Cabinet, chose the head of the newest Cabinet agency, the Department of Transportation, early. Rep. Brock Adams of Washington, a sponsor of Amtrak, may be a symbol that the trains will run on time in the Carter administration.

The one appointment that seemed based most on political reward is the Cabinet seat least patronage-laden, least independent and most

'I've never had so many people cussing me out and crying and sending me messages not to take this job, because of the past history of the job and the fact that it is a very difficult job.'

ANDREW YOUNG
Designated US Ambassador to the UN

REP. YOUNG

he, too, was payong off a campaign debt to a prominent figure in his campaign. Sen. Henry Cabot Lodge of Massachusetts who had just been defeated for re-election by a young congressman, John F. Kennedy.

Eisenhower said his aim was to upgrade American

United Nations seemed to regain some of its political appeal.

Moynihan is now a senator-elect from New York after having made a ntion of 'telling off th

World" to the delight lions of Americans.

The Third World are presumably the uents whom Young be addressing in t reassert the Ameri as a champion of tional morality. But UN ambassadors ha before him, the h cerns of defense po tegic agreements and other major foreign policy a made with heav from the US miss United Nations.

Moynihan's su the United Natic Pennsylvania G W. Scranton, s Carter that he n American to ed Nations, bu himself has illusions that tions holds a ce US foreign poli

Young, who il rights a

New York Post
FOUNDED BY ALEXANDER HAMILTON IN 1801

30. (MAGAZINE PAGE FOUR)

DOROTHY SCHIFF	Editor-in-Chief and Publisher
ADELE HALL SWEET	Assistant Publisher	PAUL SANN	Executive Editor
JAMES A. WECHSLER	Editorial Page Editor	ROBERT SPITZLER	Managing Editor

Published daily except Sunday. Owned by the New York Post Corporation, 210 South St., New York, N.Y. 10002. Dorothy Schiff, President. Adele Hall Sweet, Vice President. Byron S. Greenberg, Treasurer. Jean Gillette, Secretary.

Ambassador Young . . .

Of President-elect Carter's three new top appointments, his choice of Rep. Andrew Young (D-Ga.) as ambassador to the United Nations is clearly the most dramatic and memorable.

The fact that Young is the first black

As he has candidly acknowledged, he was not unmindful of the melancholy experiences of some of his notable predecessors when he agreed to accept the post. Adlai Stevenson and Arthur Goldberg were to learn that the promises of policy-making roles for the UN ambas-

The Washingto
AN INDEPENDENT NEW

The Young Appo

YOUNG (D-Ga.) is unquestionably ing, and perhaps even the most e to Mr. Carter's foreign policy we mean no slight to Secretary us Vance or to Prof. Zbigniew action as White House national announced yesterday, together g. But Mr. Brzezinski is a familohnson administration service lite academic output. He not

12/17

one wit black pr white ra Young for a fa domest the gro naming

Wha Young black

WHY WOULD YOU LEAVE a secure job in Congress to go to the United Nations?

Coretta King asked me not to leave. My relationship with President Carter started when there seemed to be the verge of a gun battle in Crawfordsville, and he called me and he said he had made the statement that segregation is over when he was inaugurated as governor. When we talked to him about voter registration, he said the easiest thing for him to do is deputize every high school principal in Georgia so that every high school graduate will graduate as a registered voter. And he did that.

I was amazed that he had come through on everything we asked him about. And then he called me and said, "How are you with the black community in Crawfordsville?" There were some threats to have an armed conflict, so the white community went out and bought guns. Then the black community went out and bought guns. Jimmy Carter said as governor that he was going to talk to whites personally to get rid of those guns, and he asked if I could do the same with the Black community. I said I could. And we made sure that we got rid of the guns.

But the fact that the governor himself was negotiating with the Klan types about guns was very impressive. And then a couple of times he invited me out to the governor's mansion to play tennis. The second time he invited me out, he said he'd like me to be his ambassador to the United Nations. You couldn't say no to something like that. I was a lifelong fan of Ralph Bunche, who may be more of a hero to me than Martin Luther King was, and Bunche was a hero to King. And I knew about the UN and I knew about Eleanor Roosevelt and the Declaration of Human Rights. I knew more about the UN than I did anything else.

UNITED NATIONS: When Carter asked me to go to the United Nations, I knew a lot of its people before I got there. I did not know the Indian ambassador, but he knew that I was a disciple of Gandhi. He called R.K. Sehgal and asked if he would come to New York and introduce us. He became my mentor. He had been at the UN since Bunche, as a young diplomat from India.

I had the best of advisers. Back then, there were nineteen different clearances in the State Department that you had to go through to change one word in a resolution. I never could have gotten anything done that way. I would call President Carter and ask him what he thought. And then I'd call Secretary of State Cyrus Vance and say, "I just talked to the president and this is all right with him. Is it okay with you?" Of course, he would say yes, and then I would change the resolution. But then I made nineteen people mad because I was not going through the protocol. That was why we were effective. President Carter would always pull rank on the State Department.

When I wanted to go to the meeting in Southern Africa against apartheid, the United States had not been going to those meetings. There was the idea that it was a slippery slope and we should stay out of it. The U.S. didn't want to make South Africa mad. Well, I wanted to make South Africa mad. I didn't care what happened to South Africa. I wanted to try to deal with the apartheid question. I asked President Carter if I should go? It was diplomacy as I liked it. Everybody looked out for me. I was treated royally by everybody but the press. I understood the world and so did Jimmy Carter. And that was one of the clashes, because the State Department was still under the influence of Kissinger and the Cold War.

Left: Young's confirmation hearing January 25, 1977, flanked by Georgia Senators Herman Talmadge and Sam Nunn on Capitol Hill.

Bottom Right: Andrew Young and Coretta Scott King at the United Nations General Assembly, September 20, 1977.

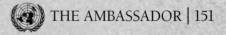

When Jimmy Carter asked me to go to the UNITED NATIONS, I knew a lot of these people already before I got there.

One other high point that changed my relationship with the Chinese was when they came, the People's Republic of China had never been to the United Nations before. They wouldn't speak English and nobody at the UN cocktail party knew what to talk to them about. They started talking about Chinese food and Chinese restaurants in New York, and it was embarrassing. My wife Jean got disgusted and went over and sat by herself.

The head of the Chinese delegation, seeing a pretty woman sitting alone, went and sat down next to her. He asked, "Where do you find good Georgia food? She said, "At my house. When are you coming to dinner?"

It was just that simple. I said, baby, there's no Georgia food in the Waldorf. And she said, don't worry. My mother's driving up from Alabama. That's close enough.

Her mother, who was in her late seventies, drove up from Alabama with a station wagon full of slow-smoked ribs she had in a freezer. She had chickens. Corn on the cob from her yard. Greens. Black-eyed peas. She went down to the Waldorf Astoria kitchen and made the cornbread, cooked the greens, fried the chicken, and warmed the ribs that had been smoked in Alabama. The Waldorf waiters served them on silver trays and the entire Chinese delegation came to dinner at the Waldorf Astoria. We served them mint juleps. It was a great success. Our guests ate everything. Normally at these UN dinners you were done by 9:30 p.m. and they toast each other's countries and leave. Instead of doing that, the Chinese got another drink. I threw a pillow on the floor and flopped down on the floor. And everybody took pillows off the couches and threw them on the floor. We stretched out on the floor and drank mint juleps and talked politics. But I never had a Chinese veto. I never had a Russian veto, because the same kind of thing I was doing with the Chinese I was doing with the Russians and with the Egyptians and with the Caribbeans. We made our house a home. One of the things the Egyptian ambassador said to me was, "When we come to your house, we feel like we are part of your family."

Left: On January 30, 1977, Supreme Court Justice Thurgood Marshall swears in Andrew Young as the first African American to serve as United States Ambassador to the United Nations. First Lady Rosalynn Carter, President Jimmy Carter, and Jean Childs Young observe the ceremony.

JIMMY CARTER JUST HAD A RESPECT
for everybody. He wasn't the least bit uncomfortable.

I remember when I invited him to meet with the Congressional Black Caucus. They didn't want to meet with him. "I ain't meeting with no Georgia cracker. Why you want to waste my time? He can't be the president, so why you want to drag him up here? I said, I met with your friends and you all have to meet with my friends. Barbara Jordan backed me up.

Jimmy Carter came into a room of nineteen of us. We were cramped in there, but he came in there and was so relaxed, so at ease. The only person he really knew was Yvonne Burke from California, and he walked over and kissed her. He disagreed with everything they asked him, and Charlie Rangel said, "Well, what the hell are you doing here if you don't agree with anything we want to do? How come you think we're going to vote for you?"

Carter said he came to tell us who he was and what he believed in, "and I hope you will vote for me." Rangel asked Carter how many Black folks he had on his staff and Carter didn't know.

Now every liberal candidate had at least one Black staff member, except the most liberal candidate who was looking for one. Charlie was furious and tried to leave. I grabbed him and I sat him down and I went to the door and I brought in Ben Brown and asked him how many black staffers they had on the campaign. He said, "Right now we just have twenty-seven and they do what everybody else does in the campaign." And Ben Brown was apologetic about it and said there will be more.

We were stunned. That shut them up.

Left: Andrew Young meets with President Carter in the Oval Office.

Right: President Jimmy Carter addressed United Nations officials, employees, and the press at the UN on October 4, 1977. Joining him were (from left) Secretary of State Cyrus Vance), UN Ambassador Andrew Young, and National Security Advisor Zbigniew Brzezinski.

I MET HARRY OPPENHEIMER, who was the richest man in South Africa. I was speaking in New York and I said that anytime a hundred businessmen agree on something, they can change any government.

ON SOUTH AFRICA

He came up to me afterwards and asked if I thought that could apply in South Africa? I told him that I didn't know South Africa, but I doubt that any government could stand up against one hundred of the strongest businessmen in the country.

I had been to South Africa maybe three or four times before I went back as ambassador. And when I went back as ambassador, the State Department wanted me to meet with only black leaders. I said, no. I said, most of them are my friends. They visited me when they came to Atlanta, I've been to visit them in their homes. I was going to parties with them when I was in Congress.

But I asked, who's the meanest son-of-a-bitch you've got to deal with? They said P. W. Botha. I said, well, why can't I meet with him? They said you don't want to meet with him, we don't talk to him. I said you should, he can't be any worse than the folk that I grew up with in Louisiana and Georgia. I picked up the phone, dialed him, and told him that it was suggested by President Carter that I pay a courtesy call to you.

He said, you come alone. I drove up to his office and just walked in to see him. And he was a little rougher than most of the folk I grew up with. He didn't even shake my hand. I walked in his office and he slammed the door behind me because he didn't want anybody else to see. He didn't even tell me to sit down. He asked, "Why did white people vote for you?"

He couldn't figure it out. I said, "I don't know, but they knew me, I had worked with them on other things, and I guess they figured we were going to have to learn to work together eventually. And they just as well start out, trying out, see how it works with me." His only answer was a grunt.

His second question was about the extent of intermarriage. I really had one or two friends that were in interracial marriages, but I said, "There's no widespread interracial marriage in Atlanta right now. Now what might happen in twenty years, I don't know. But right now, I don't know too many interracial couples. And he grunted again.

And he said, "How long do you think we have before the blood bath?" I asked, "What blood bath?" And he stood up and got very agitated and blurted, "Surely one of these days, surely one day soon, these black people are going to rise up and kill us all."

I said I didn't think that would happen. He got very angry. I said Gandhi lived here and Gandhi went back to India and Gandhi set India free of the British. And I don't think a single Englishman was killed by an Indian. That kind of calmed him down.

I said I don't know Nelson Mandela because he's been in jail. But I know everybody around him, and I have never, ever heard anyone talk about a blood bath. That's why President Carter wanted me to talk to you. He grew up in an area of Georgia that was 80 percent black. That's just about like you here. And he got along very well with his black neighbors and friends. He worked with us and his campaigns and he sent me to tell you that he has had experience dealing with racial problems. He would be glad to help you personally if you are seeking a multi-racial democracy. He could help you personally and would make the full services of the United States government available to this process.

Botha was stunned. He just grunted and never answered me. He stood up and I stood up and he started walking to the door and he let me out. And that was it. But I answered his three most significant questions. And he did call the White House and he arranged for someone with the South African government to meet with Vice President Mondale in Portugal a few weeks later. And that's what started the process of independence without violence in South Africa.

Left: Andrew Young at his station at the UN.

Left: Andrew and Jean Young were greeted by a delegation from the Dominican Republic in 1977.

Inset: Ambassador Andrew Young and Jean Young deplane.

Facing Page: Ambassador Andrew Young addresses the UN Assembly at the United Nations building in New York City.

THE ☀ SUN

A16

BALTIMORE, SATURDAY, DECEMBER 18, 1976

WILLIAM F. SCHMICK, JR., Publisher • PAUL A. BANKER, Managing Editor • J.R.L. STERNE, Editorial Page Editor

Mr. Carter's U.N. Ambassador

Representative Andrew Young will bring to the United Nations an intellect, moral purpose, a negotiating talent, and sociability. These are gifts which would in time have made him a major figure in Congress, and also those of a diplomat. He has been interested in areas of foreign policy that suffered from neglect until recently in official Washington, but not in the broad range of world affairs. A large staff at the U. S. mission has made up this gap in the backgrounds of other political appointees.

The United States has done so much preaching at the United Nations over three decades that it makes a certain sense to send a genuine preacher to do the job. A move from minority

helped him get nominated and elected. And they may expect this symbolic gesture to be followed by substantive gestures in their direction.

The United Nations has evolved from a comparatively civilized arena of the cold war into a complex forum for relations between the rich nations and poor ones. Representative Parren J. Mitchell spoke of Mr. Young as providing a bond between Africans and Afro-Americans, but the job is much more than that, for the permanent representative must link all of this country, and its policies to all of the world.

Calling this a cabinet-level job is a mild fraud that Mr. Carter inherited from previous Presidents. The ambassador at the United N

Left: Andrew Young in Switzerland in June 30, 1977.

Left: Andrew Young and Mozambique President Samora Moisés Machel.

Right Top: Andrew Young with Egyptian officials.

Right: Andrew Young addresses the special UN Conference on Rhodesia and Namibia, May 19, 1977.

UNITED NATIONS INTERNATIONAL CONFERENCE IN SUPPORT OF THE PEOPLES OF ZIMBABWE AND NAMIBIA

CONFERENCE INTERNATIONALE DES NATIONS UNIES POUR LE SOUTIEN AUX PEUPLES DU ZIMBABWE ET DE LA NAMIBIE

CONFERÊNCIA INTERNACIONAL DAS NAÇÕES UNIDAS PARA APOIO AOS POVOS DO ZIMBABWE E DA NAMÍBIA

Background Image: The UN Security Council discussing Kuwait's proposed resolution recognizing the Palestinians' right to sovereign statehood. The photo depicts Israeli Ambassador Yehuda Blum addressing the Council, with UN Ambassador Andrew Young listening.

Left: Ambassador Young talks with President Julius Nyerere in Dar Es Salaam, Tanzania.

Left Bottom: Ambassador Young meeting with Israeli Ambassador Yehuda Blum, October 1978.

Right: Ambassador Young speaking at the African Conference.

Right Bottom: Nigerian Foreign Minister to the UN Joseph Nanven Garba (*center*).

Left: Ambassador Young makes a point during an August 16, 1977, joint press conference in Barbados. With Young were Minister of External Affairs Henry deB. Forde; Don Blackman, Permanent Representative of Barbados to the United Nations; and Frank Ortiz, U.S. Ambassador to Barbados.

MR CLARK

MR GARBA

Top Left: Andrew Young speaks to a reporter.

Below: Andrew Young talking with Tugay Ulucevik of Turkey, New York, May 23, 1978.

Left Bottom: Page from *Jet* magazine interview with First Lady Rosalynn Carter, President Jimmy Carter, and Jean Young.

a trouble spot and we haven't had that kind of commitment before. . . .

JET: Will you limit your concerns to South Africa?

Young: The potential wealth of Black Africa and the resources of Black Africa are just so superior in the long run to South Africa that in order to continue to do business in all of Africa, Corporate America is going to have to do better by Blacks in South Africa.

JET: What nation in Africa poses the biggest challenge?

Young: Nigeria now is a very wealthy nation. It's the largest Black nation in the world. They are one of the largest suppliers to the United States of oil (crude oil), and they are quite wealthy now. They have given more to African Development Fund than the United States and Arabs put together, up to now. . . .

JET: Are the major n____ tional corporations ex____ Nigeria?

Young: Nigeria, first____ was getting 15 percent of ____ revenues. If they had fou____ 15 percent, cut off the ____ everything, there would h____ an invasion. They got t____ engineers to learn a lit____ about the business to t____ where they could run ____ selves and gradually the____ to get the European engi____ and they began to take ____ pumps. And once they ____ strength to run it then ____ little bit they went up t____ cent. And they ran it t____ got a little stronger ther____ up to 60 percent. . . . If ____ enter into a relationsh____ you can share in the dev____ tal process where grad____ build up your resources ____ can control your own____ you're probably better ____

UN Ambassador and Mrs. Young are greeted by President and ____ Carter and U. S. Chief of Protocol Shirley Temple Black (c) dur____ House reception.

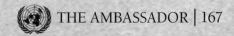

EVERYTHING THAT I WAS DOING
at the UN was totally transparent.

GOING HOME

But what I found out later was that they knew that Secretary of State Vance was having some problems with his heart and had decided that he would not serve a final year. He was going to resign after Christmas of 1979. I think there was fear that Jimmy Carter might decide for political reasons he'd want me to be secretary of state. It wasn't something I was interested in. I don't think I was ready for it. I certainly wasn't ready to tangle with the State Department for another few years.

I was happy and content.

I had a very good relationship with everybody at the UN; there was nobody that I didn't get along with. But the press was still thinking of foreign policy in Kissinger's terms. And Carter had changed that but the State Department hadn't changed.

I didn't ask anybody's advice, not even Jean's. I just sat down and wrote my letter of resignation and let her read it. And she said, that's probably best. There was no argument. And then I took it not to President Carter but to Secretary Vance because Carter probably wouldn't have wanted it. Carter said, "Why did you take it to him? I appointed you." I said I didn't want you to reject it. I knew Vance would accept it because the State Department was anxious to get rid of me.

I was ready to come back home to Atlanta. It was exactly the right time. Maynard Jackson's term was coming to an end. I wasn't thinking about being mayor. I don't know what I was thinking about, but Jean was ready to get back to Atlanta.

On Page 169: President Carter and Ambassador Young flank UN Secretary-General Kurt Waldheim during the signing of the International Covenants on Human Rights, October 1977. Looking over Carter's shoulder was Eric Suy, Under Secretary-General Legal Counsel, and looking over Young's was William B. Buffum, Under Secretary-General for Political and General Affairs).

Left: Young on a Newsweek cover posted on a door in SoHo, New York City, April 1978. Right: Young enjoys his last days at the UN.

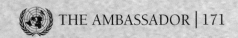

THE WHITE HOUSE
WASHINGTON

9-4-79

To Mrs. Daisy F. Young

I was grieved by your letter.

I share your regard for Andy, and I also share much of your love for him. He is, indeed, admirable in every way, and serves our nation admirably. We have every right to be proud of him.

Andy made the decision to resign and, as you say, it may be God's way for him to serve even more greatly. I believe that Andy would agree with this.

THE WHITE HOUSE
WASHINGTON

You have my best wishes and my thanks for raising such a fine son. He and Jean will be spending the night with us tonight at the White House. You must know that our close friendship is intact.

Love,

Jimmy Carter

THE WHITE HOUSE

Mrs. Daisy F. Young
2224 Cleveland Avenue
New Orleans, Louisiana 70119

MEN OF THE M✶VEMENT

C.T. VIVIAN • JOHN LEWIS • JOSEPH LOWERY • ANDREW YOUNG • HANK AARON

PRESIDENTIAL MEDAL OF FREEDOM RECIPIENTS

Andrew Young, ribboned by President Jimmy Carter.
Note: The President spoke at 3:05 p.m. in the East Room at the White House. January 16, 1981

Left page: *Men of the Movement photo: November 26, 2013*
(left to right) C. T. Vivian, John Lewis, Joseph Lowery, Andrew Young, and Hank Aaron.
© 2021 Photo: J.D. Scott

Andrew Young brought to diplomatic service a lifetime of dedication to human rights. He helped restore trust in the United States among Third World nations, especially in Africa, demonstrating to them that American foreign policy was based on our firm belief in justice, freedom, majority rule, and opportunity for all people.

I first heard about Andrew Young when I read news reports that he was in jail along with Martin Luther King, Jr., and when I saw his photographs in the newspaper seeking, with danger to his own life, to prove that our Constitution and the rulings of Earl Warren and Judge Tuttle ought to be put into effect by human beings. He's a man of quiet demeanor, having served as a United States Congressman from my State.

When I was elected President, one of my major goals was to enhance human rights and to strengthen the ties of friendship and understanding and mutual respect between our Nation and the small, sometimes weak, new nations of the world, those whose people might be black or brown or yellow and who in the past had sometimes distrusted our country because there was a lack of understanding on our own leaders' part of them. I asked Andy Young to leave the Congress and to serve as our U.N. Ambassador. He did it reluctantly. But when he went to the United Nations he served our Nation superbly.

Sometimes I have to admit I was surprised by some of the statements that Andy made, and I don't agree with all of them and didn't then. But if you listen closely to what he says, in the context of his statement, you see the wisdom and the continued purpose of his life expressed not just locally or domestically, but internationally.

Throughout the Asian countries, the South American countries, the African countries, and many others, Andy Young is the brightest star in the American firmament. He's the man who represents integrity and understanding, humility, purpose, and who exemplifies the quiet teachings of his Saviour, whom he represents as a preacher of the gospel. He's carried on well along with Coretta and others the heritage of Martin Luther King, Jr., and I'm deeply grateful for what Andy has meant to me personally, to me as President, and to our Nation. His beneficial service will help our Nation in many years ahead, and he's done it always with humility and with a quiet sense of calm, because he was sure that what he did was right for others. I've never known a person more unselfish than Andrew Young. And the respect that he enjoys around the world is well-deserved.

I'm honored to present the Medal of Freedom to Ambassador, former Congressman, great American, Andrew Young.

Swim Star

Dr. King's Top Aide Refuses White House Position

A potentially power[ful] job as deputy direc[tor of the] White House Confe[rence on Civil] Rights was polite[ly] down by the Rev. A[ndrew Young,] executive director [of Dr.] King's Southern [Leadership] Conference (SCLC) [civil] rights strategist, [declin-] ing the offer to spec[ify a pres-]ing ...

Young ... ant for civil rights Lee White. In th[e] mitted he was flattered by the off[er] has so few staff that our projects [in] the South and proposed economic [reali-] need every available man if we ar[e] tizing before the national conscie[nce] the White House conference is and pray that our (SCLC's) acti[vities] a small complement to the [White House] anticipate for the conference [that] [for the spring, will draw] [the] nation to grapple [with] [will persist.]

Andrew Young

Zimbabwe Policy Pays Off

WASHINGTON — The president's best investment of the past four years has just begun to pay off. The visit of Zimbabwe's Prime Minister Robert Mugabe sparked an enthusiasm in black America that may well rekindle the fires that Jimmy Carter so desperately needs for re-election.

Here is a president, being questioned by the liberal wing of his own party for sup-

domestic political scene.

The U.S. investment in the process of Zimbabwe's independence has been essentially in education and diplomacy.

In education, the missionary schools, and churches, together with the Kennedy administration's African scholarship program, made a healthy commitment that laid a solid foundation of skills and leadership in Zimbabwe. Mugabe's victory at the polls was led by a remarkable group of young men and women. Thirty of his close associates received Ph.D. degrees from U.S. universities. More than 4,000 Zimbabweans studied in England and America and are now ready to assist in their ...

American Journal / Richard Reeves

AMERICA'S MOST POWERFUL BLACK MAN

...If Carter becomes president, Andy Young will prob[ably have] more direct influence than any black American in hist[ory]

CBS projected Jimmy Carter as the [w]inner of the Ohio primary and a [b]lack politician turned to a friend and [sa]id: "Well, that's it. Andy Young is [the top] nigger."

That's about right. Andrew Young, [th]e U.S. representative from the Fifth [d]istrict of Georgia, the first black elec[t]ed to Congress from the South since [Re]construction, Congregationalist min[ist]er, Martin Luther King's top assis[ta]nt, and Jimmy Carter's friend and [a]dviser, is already an impor[ta]nt and very impressive man.

[If] Jimmy Carter becomes [pr]esident, Andy Young will [pr]obably have more direct [in]fluence on government than [an]y black American in his[to]ry.

[The] thing that strikes you [in tal]king to Young about all [th]at is how Southern he is— [an]d it's not just that he likes [to] talk about how to make ...

When he first came north to attend Hartford Theological Seminary in the middle-1950s, Young found that he was more comfortable with white Southern classmates than with more liberal Northerners. He still sounds a little that way when he talks about black-white alliances in the South and his tolerance of George Wallace as part of the Carter coalition: "We've had a lot of experience with converted bigots and we know we can trust them.

... [be]ing these days that [be]ing the center of the [black] Americans it [close] to that for a [a third] of the nation [were] educated in [colleges and universi] Atlanta. It is the [Du]Bois, Walter Whit[e] [Whitney] Young, ... Julian Bond. The ... it's called, and A[ndy] black ... tell hi[m] ... [admi]nistration pushe[d] [At]lanta ...

Young sees future filled with hope for black progress

By BOB R...

REP. ANDREW YOUNG of Atlanta in town for the [se]cond time since his election last November stands [wit]h Vincent Malveaux, president of Community Or[ganization] for Urban Politics (left) and Robert [Collin]s, magistrate judge of Criminal District [Court.] Rep. Young spoke at COUP's third annual [dinner] last Friday at the Marriott Hotel. COUP's [officers] and board members were installed at [the same] time with Judge Collins administering the [oath of] office. Young, a freshman Congressman and [a native] of New Orleans, will ...

Young Claims FBI Informed Opponent

BY MAURICE FLIESS
Journal Washington Bureau

WASHINGTON — Rep. Andrew Young of Atlanta says he has evidence that the FBI supplied information about him to his opponent in the 1970 election, then-Rep. Fletcher Thompson.

Young said here Tuesday that after his move into the Atlanta congressional office vacated by Thompson in 1972, his staff came across a series of memos the FBI had sent to the Thompson campaign.

The memos were discovered in boxes of ...

concentrated on such things as the content of addresses Young had been making around the country, and his schedule of speaking engagements.

"I never realized (in 1970) that I was running against the FBI, too," Young said.

Young made the disclosure shortly after a former FBI agent testified here that his superiors in 1970 had asked him to obtain a sample of Young's handwriting.

Now retired from the bureau, Arthur Murtagh told the House Intelligence Com...

[w]as consulted on every major Carter decision

[No]t just an intellectual commitment [to] them. They proved themselves in [per]sonal struggle, often against fam[ily] [an]d tradition. . . . They don't chick[en ou]t and some people do when it [come]s to housing in New York and [Bosto]n."

Church ... of th[e] ... Conf[erence] ... execu[tive] ... ran f[rom] ... to R[e] ... serve ...

[Gentle re... by women ... ay to ju[stice]

civil rights activist [na]tional convention of [w]here Monday night [a] "gentle revolu-

[Ro]bert George Vosbe[rg]

THE ONLY PROBLEM I HAD was with the press. One day, I was walking across the street from the UN when an Associated Press reporter said to me, 'you don't think that South Africa is a legitimate government, do you?'

Once, Mayor Ivan Allen asked me to come see him and he taught me the most valuable lesson in my struggle to become a political figure.

He told me that he went to high school with Jack Tarver, later publisher and editor of the Atlanta Journal-Constitution, and that their wives played bridge together every week. He said he couldn't get a decent story out of the paper unless he went over and sat down with the whole editorial board and explained what he was trying to do. Then he had to get all the City Hall writers to come to his office and tell them again. And when the story came out, they still didn't get it right.

But he said, "You can't run a city if the press doesn't understand what you're trying to do." I never forgot that.

I had pretty good press as a congressman because I talked with the press a lot, and then I had bad press at the United Nations because I talked to the press a lot but always told the truth. Half the time, the State Department didn't want anybody to tell the truth, so the things that I said were just factual. For instance, when someone asked, "You don't think South Africa is a legitimate government, do you?" and I said, "Uh-uh"—that's all I said!—the headline would read, "Young Says South Africa Illegitimate Government."
Well, that won me a lot of friends at the United Nations because everyone there knew it was an illegitimate government.

The thing is, when I'd get trapped into these things, I never backed out of them. I always stood up for myself. I said you have 15 percent of the people who vote and who own all the property, who are the only ones entitled to education and first-class health care. I said, you cannot have a democracy if only 15 percent of the people are involved and protected. I said, the Asians, nor the Coloreds, nor the Blacks are part of the government and have any legitimacy. So that's what kept it controversial. But I never had any corrections from President Carter.

So, dealing with the press is one of the most important skills you have to master in politics.

The Story of a Struggle: 'From King to Congress'

By William Gildea

From King to Congress" new film telling how the black man was elected ongress from the deep in 100 years.

subject is Rep. An- Young (D-Ga.), a for- ide to the late Dr. Luther King Jr., and ovie was shown last at the Kennedy Cen- an audience of about nding a Capitol Hill

added, noting that Young had brought together a coalition of blacks and whites, young and old to win.

Mrs. King said she hoped the 52-minute film would be shown on national television, in classrooms and to community groups. And this is exactly the kind of exposure the filmmakers hope for. Already it has been shown on television in a number of cities and will be seen locally on Channel 5

pened a lot in 1974," Young said as he greeted guests. "People with limited resources, showing you can win. We were sort of two years ahead."

In an uphill campaign in Atlanta and its suburbs, with a 57 per cent white population, Young literally ran for office, racing up and down streets shaking hands and pleading for votes in an intense effort at personal contact. His workers were

THE MAYOR

Now We Need You

I've got **Young** ideas

AFTER TRYING AND FAILING IN 1970 TO WIN A SEAT IN CONGRESS, YOUNG WAS APPOINTED BY ATLANTA MAYOR SAM MASSELL TO THE CITY'S COMMUNITY RELATIONS COMMISSION.

The position gave Young political credibility in the city, while sharpening his reputation as a negotiator.

In 1981, after being urged by a number of people, including incumbent Mayor Maynard Jackson and Coretta Scott King, the widow of Martin Luther King Jr., Young ran for mayor of Atlanta. He was elected with 55 percent of the vote and was re-elected in 1985 with nearly 85 percent of the vote.

As the fifty-fifth mayor of Atlanta, Young spent a lot of time across the country and abroad building Atlanta's reputation as a financial competitor. The New Orleans-born Young was instrumental in building a new Atlanta. He championed the development of Hartsfield International Airport, which became the world's busiest. During Young's tenure, the city of Atlanta attracted more than 1,000 new businesses, while collecting more than $70 billion in private investment and more than a million new jobs to the region. He helped salvage plans for the Georgia Dome and set in motion plans to bring back Underground Atlanta back to useful retail and entertainment life.

As mayor, Young brought the 1988 Democratic National Convention to Atlanta. Then he set his sights on bringing the world to Atlanta.

YOUNG for **Atlanta**

360 Spring Street, N.W.
Atlanta, Georgia 30308

Tel. 404/659-2639

Jesse Hill, Jr.
Co-Chair

R. Charles Loudermilk
Co-Chair and Treasurer

October 26, 1981

Statement by Andrew Young

PUBLIC SAFETY:
Partnership Between Public Safety Officers
And the Communities They Serve

Public safety affects the quality of life of every citizen in our city and impacts substantially on commercial activity. Atlantans have the right to feel safe and to be safe in ther places of business.

Young

A Leader for Atlanta

Elect Andrew Young Mayor

360 Spring St., N.W.   Telephone 659-2639

You've HEARD ALL THE THINGS I'VE DONE or tried to do, but none have been as much fun, or as successful, or where I feel we have accomplished as much, than being the mayor of Atlanta.

When I came back from the UN, the business community that had decided to support Maynard, and worked very well with him for eight years, would all have said that he was a good mayor. But for some reason, they suddenly decided that people wouldn't invest in cities led by black mayors. Newark and Gary and Cleveland were trotted out as cities that were dying because they had black mayors. In Atlanta, that line of political and business leadership blamed everything going on around the country on Black mayors, and they did not want another Black mayor in Atlanta.

That is why people like Maynard and Belafonte wanted me to run, but I didn't want to be mayor. I was tired of politics and tired of the strain. We were flat broke. We didn't have a bank account when I left the UN. At that time, the mayor's salary was $50,000 a year. I had a daughter in law school, one in engineering school, one just beginning college, a son waiting in the wings, and I didn't see how I could live on $50,000 a year and get them through school. I also knew that federal money was running short. Ronald Reagan was president and I knew he wasn't going to give Atlanta any money, because he wasn't giving any cities money. He was trying to take money away from cities. I figured being mayor meant that I would end up having to lay off all my friends and have everyone in the civil rights movement, that I had helped train, out picketing me, and I'd be broke. So there was nothing exciting about becoming mayor at that time. In no uncertain terms, I said there was no way I would consider running for mayor.

Well, Maynard set up this big meeting. A lady in her eighties was there, Sister Susie LaBord. I don't know whether Maynard had put her up to this, but I was sitting there, and she took her walking stick and shook it in my face. She said, "When you came here, you wasn't nothing. And we done made something out of you."

I told her that Martin Luther King Jr. made me. She said, "We made him too! We sent you to Congress. Sent you to the United Nations. You been all over the world. Now we need you and you ain't got time for us. We done wasted our time on you." And she turned and walked out of the room and slammed the door so hard that I thought the windows were going to break.

Sister LaBord was the moral authority, and after that encounter I said I guessed I was running. I went to Charlie Loudermilk because he'd been a good friend and told him that I needed him to support me. Because what happens if I win, and nobody has supported me? They're going to be enemies for life. I said, I need you with me so that if I win, we can bring them all back in, because they are all your friends. And on that basis, he agreed to support me.

One thing I knew was that the U.S. economy was terribly inflationary. It was going to be very hard to get investment in, to grow here. But people from all over the world needed a safe place to invest. And while the U.S. was an inflationary economy, it was also the biggest market in the world. For Atlanta to survive, it had to become an international city. I had the connections for that, and I had the notoriety.

At the end of the day, being mayor was the most exciting job I've ever had. The excitement didn't quit when I was no longer mayor, because everybody's always calling on me to do something.

Andrew Young served as Atlanta's mayor from 1982 until 1990, ushering in a new era of business growth. During his tenure, private investments into the city exploded, creating a construction boom that also included the expansion of the Atlanta airport. It all set Atlanta up as a major international city.

The Five Mayors: Andrew Young kept good company with each of the still-living mayors, including Ivan Allen, Sam Massell, Bill Campbell, and Maynard Jackson.

Jean Young
Now that was
a Woman!
Jean Young

Did you
see the
angels?

Yes, Angels

There is one
that stays
beside her

fundamental

Every Child
Can Learn

March on Selma

Elementary
School Teacher
Atlanta
Public Schools

PARENTS

YOUNG

She touched
the lives
of children
from her home
and neighborhood
across America
and across
the globe.
Andrew Young

Jean Young
was a woman
from whom shone
an inner light
of love,
commitment
and service
to her family,
the children
of the world
and all of
humankind.
Marian Wright Edelman

Habitat for Humanity

FIRST LADY OF ATLANTA

JEAN
CHILDS
YOUNG

LOSES HER BATTLE
WITH LIVER CANCER

ATLANTA, GEORGIA
SEPTEMBER 16, 1994

Leading an Orchestra

A YOUTHFUL ANDREW YOUNG HAD DREAMS OF RUNNING THE 200 AND 400 METER DASHES IN THE 1952 HELSINKI OLYMPICS, BUT IT WAS ONE OF LIFE'S HURDLES THAT GOT HIM.

The Games had been in Young's imagination since 1936 when, at the age of four, he met the great Olympian Jesse Owens just after the sprinter had crushed the concept of Aryan domination.

After starring on Howard University's vaunted track team, Young enrolled in the Hartford Theological Seminary, but with his sights still set on the Olympics. After his first year at Hartford, he made plans to train in New York City. But just before he was to go to New York, he got a call from the superintendent for the Convention of the South of the Congregational Church telling him that a small church in Marion, Alabama, needed a summer assistant. It paid $5 a month.

"It would not reflect well on my commitment to the ministry if I refused the first assignment that was offered to me," Young said. "Unfortunately, I would simply have to give up my dream of running in Helsinki."

Ten years later, when Young moved to Atlanta in 1961, he had to carefully navigate where his family would live because of segregation and his fear for their safety when he was traveling away from home. In 1996, forty-four years after giving up his own Olympic dreams, Young, dressed all in white for the opening ceremonies, marched into Atlanta's Olympic Stadium, having brought the XXIII Summer Games to the South.

That journey had begun in 1987, when a nervous Billy Payne approached the two-term mayor about the wild idea of bringing the Olympics to Atlanta. Young's staff didn't even want to take the meeting with Payne. Previous games had left their host cities broke, and Athens, Greece, the birthplace in 1896 of the modern Olympics, was everyone's favorite to host the centennial games.

Besides, Atlanta at the time was considered a "second-tier city," still steeped in Confederate lore and iconography, although the overriding presence of Martin Luther King Jr. and a string of Black mayors was changing that.

Young accepted the meeting. He told Payne to go for it. As co-chair of the Atlanta Committee for the Olympic Games, Mayor Young used his capital as a civil rights leader, former Congressman, and former U.N. Ambassador to help secure enough votes to win the bid over Athens.

In talking about the "Atlanta Way," and a reformed American South, Young touted the city's civil rights history and bragged about its reputation for racial harmony. He also reminded everyone who would listen about Atlanta's strong economy.

Young became a driving force in promoting Atlanta as an international city.

The Atlanta Games brought more than 10,300 athletes from 197 National Olympic Committees competing in twenty-six sports. Two dozen countries, including eleven former Soviet republics, made their Summer Olympic Games debuts in Atlanta.

Using exclusive private funding, record sponsorship deals and massive broadcasting rights, the 1996 Olympics proved profitable.

The Games also had a lasting impact on Atlanta. The building of Centennial Olympic Park led to the revitalization of downtown Atlanta and still serves as a city gathering spot. The Olympic Village buildings have been converted to college dormitories. And Centennial Olympic Stadium, after a stint as the home of the Atlanta Braves, has been retrofitted into a college football stadium that is at the heart of a revitalized Summerhill neighborhood.

Young didn't make the 1952 team, but he would later say his participation in the 1996 Olympics was "as important as anything else I've ever done."

The Olympics HAD BEEN PART OF MY BLOOD. My daddy took me to see Jesse Owens when I was four years old.

And I knew Ralph Metcalfe, who ran in the 1932 and 1936 Olympics with Owens, and Herb Douglas, who won bronze in 1948, because both coached track at Xavier University in my hometown. All of my race relations background, all of my culture and then nationalism, was tied to the Olympics. Up to the time when I was thirty, all of my thoughts about the Olympics were of me competing in the Olympics. Then when I got too old to think about that, I dreamed about visiting the Olympics.

Billy Payne was the first who suggested, "Let's bring the Olympics to us." But when he came to talk about the Olympics in 1987, Shirley Franklin, the city manager, didn't want me to even talk with him. Nobody wanted me to talk to him because they knew that Montreal, the 1976 host city, had been left $700 million in debt.

Those around me were trying to convince me that I had one more year in office and a nearly balanced budget, and I didn't need to leave the city with Olympic debt. But I talked to Tom Bradley, the former mayor of Los Angeles, which hosted the 1984 Olympics, and he told me that I could run the Olympics as a private business. Not as a government operation.

He said the problem with Montreal was that everybody thought the government had endless money. So there were cost overruns on every project. Los Angeles ran it like a business with no government money. They built very little and used stuff they already had. They knew there was a finite budget and they had to stay within it.

Atlanta didn't have any government money in the Olympics. But we had Wall Street money. Nobody thought we had a chance, but we decided we were going to host the Olympics not as a city project but as a private sector venture.

We raised $2.5 billion privately. We had the largest Olympics ever, with more countries and more athletes than ever before. We ended with a surplus of almost $100 million, and minorities and women got 41 percent of the business. But the Olympics worked because 200,000 of us worked for almost ten years as volunteers.

Atlanta's was one of the first citizen Olympics. The key to our winning the host competition was that we were already an international city. I think we had about sixty consulates here then. Maggie Womack brought me a little pamphlet that had a list of the countries that had a vote on the selection committee. There were eighty-six countries on the list.

I checked the countries where we either had a consulate in Atlanta or I knew personally the representatives. We got the Japanese companies to invite the Japanese representative here. I invited all the Africans to my house—about nineteen of them. I don't have a big house but we said we'll have a good dinner. We had Roberto Goizueta, the former chairman of Coca-Cola, who said he couldn't come out for Atlanta, but he could help me with contacts throughout Latin America.

I think there were six votes from people of Indian descent, and Atlanta businessman R. K. Sehgal, who was the chairman of Law Companies, volunteered to work on them.

When I looked down the list, I knew you needed a majority of eighty-six. I HAD CONTACTS IN FIFTY-FIVE of the eighty-six countries. To win the Olympics, it was politics.

But I, Billy Payne, Maynard Jackson, and Charlie Battle visited every country that had a vote except two that we couldn't get to because wars were going on.

The day we won the Olympics bid award, ten thousand folks emerged. UPS announced that it was moving its entire headquarters to Atlanta, including its air fleet. ING moved its headquarters to Atlanta. The hotel downtown that is now the Four Seasons—a fifty-story office building, hotel, and condos—broke ground the day we won the Olympics. People understood that the Olympics is one way to bring in money. It put us on the map and it gave us a chance to let people know that our way of doing business works.

I didn't have any shining moments in the Olympics. My shining moments were getting the Olympics. It was the Olympics, business, and culture all coming together. That is what the Olympics did.

ON TRAINING FOR THE OLYMPICS IN COLLEGE

Atlanta landing the Olympics was no redemption for me, because by that time I had heard a higher call.

Yet I am grateful for the Olympics vision. I never smoked a cigarette or took a drink the entire time I was in college. The physical fitness and the athletic discipline, you don't even need to go to the Olympics. You just need to dream about it. And it keeps you healthy if you dream about it and train like you are going to be an Olympian.

That is why I am planning to make 90.

Page 193: Andrew Young, Billy Payne, and Maynard Jackson at a press conference.

Left: Andrew Young and Maynard Jackson, boosting the Summer Games.

After Atlanta was awarded the 1996 Olympics, Young took a victory lap and began a major period of celebration throughout the city of Atlanta. On the right, he holds the Olympic Rings with Billy Payne, president and chief executive officer of the Atlanta Committee for the Olympic Games (ACOG).

DELTA SALUTES THE
ATLANTA ORGANIZING COMMITTEE
"Champions of the World"

Left: Andrew and Jean Young celebrating through downtown Atlanta.
Below Middle: Andrew Young poses with students, Atlanta, September 24, 1990.
Below Middle Right: City Council President Marvin Arrington, Atlanta, September 24, 1990.
Right Page: Maynard and Valerie Jackson and family parading through downtown, September 24, 1990.

ATLANTA ORGANIZING COMMITTEE
Volunteers

Atlanta
1996

Previous Pages: Delta Air Lines handing out Champion Medals as they celebrate on the following page. Maynard Jackson, Andrew Young and Billy Payne.

Top: Business leaders discuss the plan.

Below: On July 19, 1994, the Atlanta Committee for the Olympics Games celebrated the two-year countdown until the Games would commence.

Right: Andrew Young was excited to present Atlanta as the next Olympic City.

Next Page: Andrew Young making the torch run over the Edmund Pettus Bridge, Selma, Alabama. He transfers the flame in two cases July 1996.

Torchbearer. On the site of Bloody Sunday thirty-one years earlier, Young returned to Selma's Edmund Pettus Bridge to carry the Olympic Torch across it.

Background: Aquatic Qualifying Center and Centennial Park.

Middle: Gold Medal Ribbon.

Right: Muhammad Ali before he lights the Cauldron during the Opening Ceremonies of the 1996 Olympics on July 19, 1996.

The Andrew Young Foundation

HIGH IMPACT SUSTAINABLE SOLUTIONS ARE DIFFICULT TO ACHIEVE IN ONE GENERATION. HOWEVER, THEY NEED TO BE STARTED NOW FOR THE FUTURE GENERATIONS TO BENEFIT FROM THEM.

When I turned 75, someone asked me if I had a bucket list. It got me into thinking that I had done enough work on earth and it was about time I needed to think how to get into heaven, you see. I latched onto "feeding the hungry" to really serve the Lord.

But, as it has always happened in my life, the Lord paved the way with solutions. After my mayor's term, I was hired by "Law and Engineering" to help them make connections in Africa.

I go to Uganda and there was this dam that had been choked by this green floating plants called Duckweed. They were growing so fast and had become so thick that they stopped the turbine blades and the power plant was shut down.

While everybody was cussing about it, I said "Something that grows this fast, God must have put it for some purpose."

Few years later, I came across a Cajun in Louisiana cooking it trying to make moonshine. We collected the ashes and sent it to lab to get it tested. It came out as the most nutritious plant-based protein.

I came back to Atlanta and spoke at a Jain convention who are Hindus that are staunch vegetarians. The headline in the New York Times the previous day was "save the cows, starve the children" attacking Prime Minister Modi for not giving enough protein to children.

It was totally insensitive to the belief of people in India and I thought this could be the solution to the world's hunger problem. That gave the mission for our foundation.

Given my varied experiences over decades, we get pulled in many different directions all the time, and we try hard to be focused on our mission.

These projects have come from a real global shortage of protein, social issues, the flooding of the Mississippi River and maritime issues our nation faces today. We are undertaking these projects with a goal to help feed and empower 8.5 billion people expected on this planet by 2030.

The Andrew J. Young Foundation is a community based 501(c)(3) non-profit organization that has been built upon civil rights leader Andrew Young's philosophy of nonviolent change and a belief that unto whom much is given, much is required. Ambassador Young is a prominent speaker on the civil rights movement, diplomacy, peacekeeping and reconciliation, who is called on a daily basis by organizations around the world to share his thoughts on overcoming societal divisions on the basis of respect, inclusion and empowerment.

We are driven by the philosophy to feed the hungry, heal the sick, clothe and house the poor and set at liberty those who are oppressed. Besides actively working on civil and human rights, education and empowerment, the foundation incubates social innovations that have the potential to solve the basic needs of people living in poverty in America, Africa and across the globe. Through the following projects, the foundation is currently focused upon finding sustainable solutions for food security and fighting malnutrition, job creation, and economic development. These solutions are poised to empower undeserved populations and uplift the quality of life in the society worldwide.

Above: Aquaponics production system at the Andrew and Walter Young Family YMCA in Atlanta.

Below: Students pose as they take a break from their training on maintaining an Aquaponics system.

Right Page: Andrew Young in conversation about aquaponics with farmers from the southeast United States.

HUNGER AND NUTRITION

Aquaponics Production

The Aquaponics Project will provide food security solutions for the development of sustainable communities around food, water and energy. Aquaponics is a closed-loop controlled environment agriculture system that mimics mother nature to create a symbiotic biome environment to grow fish, organic greens, vegetables, herbs and fruits. The system is housed within a greenhouse with automated controls to produce ten times more food on the same amount of land using 5% of water used in conventional agriculture. The controlled environment allows safe and quality organic food production with produce predictability for communities and/or commercial ventures. A one-acre farm produces 1,200 pounds of organic greens and vegetables per day and over 2,000 pounds of fish per week. The foundation has assembled the best-in-class team from Australia, India and Canada, and is currently working with private entrepreneurs on developing a farm in Georgia. The farm will also have a training institute attached to it to train future farmers in this innovative farming technology who would be employed at future commercial scale farms.

The foundation designed and built a test scale aquaponics farm at the Andrew Young YMCA five years ago to help children learn about growing food. The farm supports training, and the produce is used by the YMCA to feed children. The project has helped thousands of children over the last five years. As a metric of measurement of our work, the aquaponics program at the Andrew Young YMCA exposed 200 youth to this innovative farming method while 200 pounds of fresh produce and 50 pounds of fish were distributed to local families and community residents in 2020 despite the Covid-19 pandemic. The project is currently sustained by donations received every year.

All: Duckweed Production in California and Louisiana.

THE LEMNA PROJECT AIMS TO EXTRACT RICH PLANT-BASED ORGANIC PROTEIN AND ETHANOL FROM GLOBALLY AVAILABLE TINY AQUATIC PLANTS KNOWN AS DUCKWEED OR LEMNACEAE.

The foundation is working on this idea to provide an alternative wholesome organic protein with essential amino acids to help alleviate malnutrition. The process is a closed loop production system that is sustainable with zero discharge to the environment. It will help to create jobs and empower rural communities within the United States and around the world.

Our pilot research produced about 50% protein concentrate powder with 18 essential amino acids and 19% fiber. This rare combination is better than soy, green peas or any other plant source for protein known to us. The foundation aims to mix lemna protein powder with juices, bread, cereals, among others and fight malnutrition worldwide.

Our pre-commercial phase in California grows Lemna in a controlled environment in interconnected raceways. We have developed our own harvesters and a bio-refinery system developed by Floyd Butterfield that converts Lemna into rich protein powder. We are working to raise funds to build a commercial scale bio-refinery in Georgia as a demonstration operation that could be replicated around the world to feed the hungry.

Andrew Young chats with philanthropist Dae Shin, a key sponsor of the Andy Young Foundation's hunger and nutrition programs, about how they can fight hunger through the production of the lemna plant.

Above: Walter and Andrew Young, **Below:** Ribbon-cutting ceremony.

Right: Andrew Young meets with students in Atlanta.

ANDREW AND WALTER YOUNG FAMILY YMCA

DOCUMENTARIES

ANDREW YOUNG
Presents

DOCUMENTARIES TO TELEVISION
Andrew Young is a man who has spent his formidable lifetime in front of cameras.

In the late 1950s, as Director of Youth Services at the National Council of Churches in New York, Reverend Andrew Young became a producer and occasional host of "Look Up and Live," an inspirational, Sunday morning TV program on CBS– the very first network show to feature a recurring, interracial cast. It won a prestigious Peabody Award, and far more importantly, gave him a working knowledge of the television industry. That's why, just a few years later when he joined the Civil Rights movement, he was able to give keen advice to Dr. Martin Luther King, Jr., about media strategy– right down to what time of day to hold a press conference in order to give reporters enough time to get their film developed for the nightly news.

In all his political roles, but perhaps never more than when he served in the United Nations, Ambassador Young faced those same cameras almost daily, deftly fielding questions with crisp, honest answers that on occasion were too candid for some.

At the age of seventy-five, in 2007, his relationship with television came full circle as co-creator and host of the important educational documentary series "Andrew Young Presents" –never imagining it would still be on the air when his ninetieth birthday rolled around, thanks to the foundation he chairs.

In 2011, at a special ceremony in New York, the National Academy of Television Arts and Sciences honored Andrew Young with a rare national Emmy Award for Lifetime Achievement.

Andrew Young Presents

On one of his many trips to Africa, Andrew Young visited Rwanda and was amazed to discover a thriving, enlightened nation whose people somehow had come together in a spirit of peace and reconciliation just years after the devastation of genocide and civil war. The story was remarkable, but virtually unknown, and he was unable to convince media outlets to invest the money and resources necessary to tell it. But as Ambassador Young always says, coincidence is God's way of remaining anonymous.

A longtime television news producer named CB Hackworth, who had known Ambassador Young since he was mayor, knocked on his door to pitch what the newsman thought was a longshot idea that they join forces and produce an

ANDREW YOUNG
PRESENTS
A STORY OF RECONCILIATION AND HOPE
IN THE AFTERMATH OF GENOCIDE

RWANDA RISING

independent film. Not ten minutes into the conversation, Ambassador Young scheduled a trip to Rwanda and agreed to find the funding for a video crew. That was just the start.

Their feature length documentary *Rwanda Rising* opened the Pan African Film Festival in Los Angeles in 2007 to considerable acclaim - and that launched what would become one of the Andrew J. Young Foundation's most enduring and celebrated achievements.

Rwanda Rising became the pilot for *Andrew Young Presents,* a series of quarterly documentaries intended to tell positive stories often overlooked by the mainstream media- from prosperity on the African continent to deeply personal recollections of the civil rights movement, from guns and youth violence to up-

close-and-personal biographies of such close friends as Jimmy Carter and Henry Aaron. Ambassador Young, with Hackworth as his director and co-writer, has produced over thirty-five documentaries in fifteen years. The Emmy-winning show is seen in national syndication on over one hundred of the country's top markets and around the world on the American Forces Network.

Through this series, the foundation provides a forum that enables Ambassador Young to continue to be heard as a champion of civil and human rights while also preserving history for younger generations at a time some want to erase it, ensuring viewers will know where we have come from and where we need to go.

Top: Andrew Young in Birmingham, at the park where police unleashed dogs and fire hoses on peaceful demonstrators in 1963. He narrowly escaped harm.

Videographer Dave Dawson records Ambassador Young's arrival on one of his visits to the African continent.

Andrew and Carolyn Young join other notable figures who have planted trees in Ethiopia to fight climate change.

Crossing in St. Augustine

Andrew Young returned to Florida with his wife Carolyn and daughter Andrea to stand at the intersection where he was beaten in 1964 to recount that experience on video. That led to one of his most powerful and personal documentaries, *Crossing in St. Augustine*. It awakened viewers to an almost forgotten chapter of the Civil Rights movement and the impact locally was so great that the City of St. Augustine began to embrace that part of its buried past – even renaming the intersection Andrew Young Crossing and adding a wonderful monument in its historic Plaza de la Constitución.

KODAK SAFETY FILM

KODAK TRI X PAN FILM

2011

→18   →18A   →19   →19A   →20   →20A   →21

Andrew Young Crossing

EDUCATION:

International University of Grand-Bassam (IUGB)

IUGB was established in 2005 in Cote d'Ivoire, Africa under the guidance of Andrew Young who encouraged the relationship between Georgia State University (Andrew Young School of Public Policy) and Africa. The University has helped educate thousands of graduates and undergraduate students from Africa on student exchange programs. The university is supported by the government of Cote d'Ivoire and continues to thrive and expand. The foundation is currently helping IUGB in securing accreditation from an American University to increase the impact of degrees conferred by the university. It is our hope this process will empower students in Africa and help in rebuilding the continent.

Above: Ambassador Young speaking with student from IUGB.

Below: Anthony Jones (*l*) Ambassador Andrew Young (*m*) Dr. Mathew Daniels.

Scholarship Program for students going to HBCUs

The goal of the Andrew Young HBCU Scholarship Program is to encourage first-year students at black colleges to become champions for the nonviolent social justice principles of Martin Luther King Jr. and Ambassador Young. Launched with a generous grant from McGraw Hill Education, this program was established by Anthony Jones and Dr. Matthew Daniels to encourage a new generation to harness the powerful tools of the digital age to become future pioneers for the cause of civil rights in our nation and our world.

PROMETRA International partnership:

One of our strongest African partners is PROMETRA International which is a credible, transparent international nonprofit that has been in continuous operation for over three decades. The unique strength of PROMETRA International is its organized network of national chapters (20 African nations) that are all formally recognized by governments, maintain links to ministries, academic institutions, NGOs, but most importantly to grass roots traditional healers and indigenous leaders.

Prometra works with the Andrew J Young Foundation in three important areas:

- Scientific research on African herbal therapies in HIV and Ebola (partnerships with Morehouse School of Medicine and USMRIID)
- Development of aquaponics systems to combat food insecurity and develope income generating community-based projects throughout Africa
- Right Message, Right Messenger training of traditional healers with scientifically based curricula in the areas of HIV/AIDS, Immunization, MCH, Oral Rehydration of Infants, Public Health Sanitation, etc.

Recognizing that most Africans utilize traditional healers for health services and health education - they clearly are the right messengers. It is the work of the AYF and PROMETRA to assure that these messengers have the right message.

Top: Dr. Valerie Montgomery Rice, President of Morehouse School of Medicine, with Dr. Erick Gbodossou, President PROMETRA, Andrew Young to the right.

Below: Testing of PROMETRA medicinal plant samples at Morehouse School of Medcine.

HEALTH AND HEAL PROJECTS:

Oxygen Concentrators for India

India was reeling from a second wave of Covid-19 in April of 2021 as people were dying in thousands for lack of oxygen. Because of the pandemic, there was a global shortage of oxygen concentrators, which extract oxygen from air. A shipment of 25 of these life-saving units have been shipped by the Andrew J. Young Foundation through a global collaboration effort amid the lockdown. A consignment of concentrators reached Patna in the state of Bihar and the machines were distributed to local hospitals. Some were sent to remote areas where no other medical equipment had been available to combat the novel coronavirus.

The foundation followed the last mile approach to ensure they reached the remotest of the places. It was important to reach villages that were outside the mainstream and we chose Bihar, the place where Mahatma Gandhi started the movement for independence from British rule in 1917. We're hoping to be able to keep a supply line open. "We realize some may see this as just a drop in the bucket, but we guarantee you the people whose lives are being saved won't see it that way." says Andrew Young. The concentrators are being used to save hundreds of lives daily.

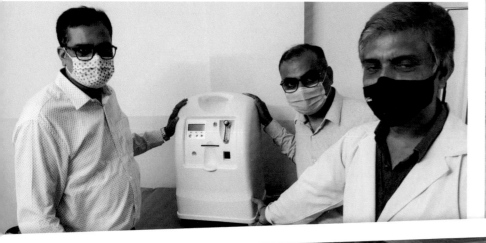

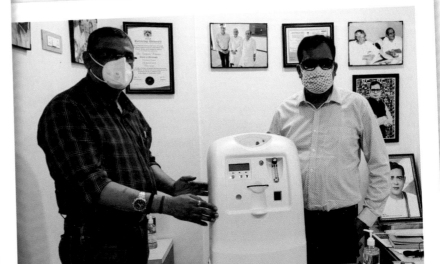

Increasing immunity for viral diseases including Covid-19: For many years, The Andrew J. Young Foundation has worked on initiatives for fighting HIV-1 and Ebola infection with Prof. Ethan W. Taylor of the University of North Carolina at Greensboro, who has been a pioneer in studies of the role of selenium in fighting viral diseases.

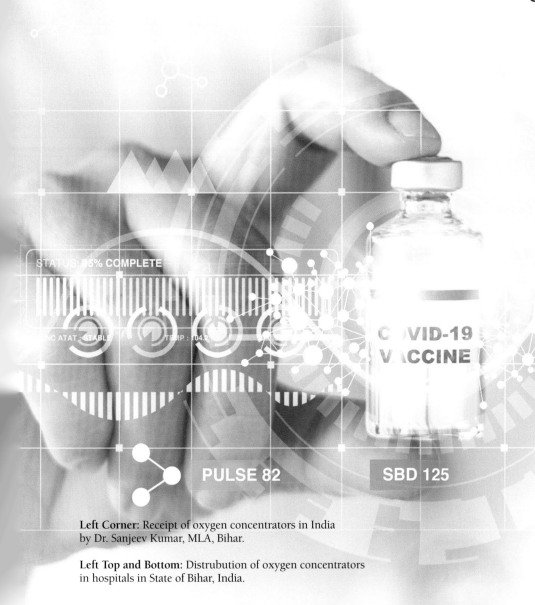

In this effort, we supplied Selenium supplements to Liberia in 2020 upon their request that were shipped from Germany. Our last involvement was in 2014 when the Ebola crisis had engulfed the country. During that time, we had arranged to send Selenium (a trace element found in Earth) tablets from the United States to Liberia which was distributed by non-profits to local people who were infected with Ebola. Without the double-blind study, empirically, the survival rate in individuals who took Selenium was found to be 66 percent as compared to 44 percent in patients who didn't take Selenium.

Left Corner: Receipt of oxygen concentrators in India by Dr. Sanjeev Kumar, MLA, Bihar.

Left Top and Bottom: Distrubution of oxygen concentrators in hospitals in State of Bihar, India.

PEACE AND RECONCILIATION PROJECT:
Atlanta Global City of Peace

Georgia has more than three hundred years of history of peace starting with Chief Tomochichi befriending General James Oglethorpe in Savannah in 1733. The civil rights movement didn't start in Atlanta in a vacuum, but stands on the legacy of this century's old pursuit to live together. Ambassador Young is the co-chair of Rodney Cook Sr. Park which opened to the public this year. The park will have the largest ensemble of statues of civil rights leaders and Nobel Peace Prize winners. Congressman John Lewis's statue was recently unveiled in the park. The park will have the statue of Tomochichi on top of a 100-foot tall column to honor the Native Americans, on whose shoulders the United States has been built. The column will house the C. T. Vivian Library and will have a peace pantheon to honor Dr. Martin Luther King Jr. and Coretta Scott King. Located on the westside of Atlanta, this park is poised to be the global center of peace which will be visited by millions of people from around the world in the future.

Top Left: Rodney Cook Sr. Peace Park in Vine City, Atlanta. Mercedes-Benz Stadium and Atlanta skyline in the background.

Below Left: Opening of the Peace Park to the public in July 2021.

Below Left Middle: Unveiling of John Lewis Statue in the Rodney Cook Sr. Peace Park, (l) Rodney Cook, Jr., President, National Monument Foundation, (m) Mayor Keisha Lance Bottoms, (r) Andrew Young.

Below: Statue of Chief Tomochichi placed in front of The Millennium Gate which will be placed on top of a 115-foot-tall column in the Peace Park.

ECONOMIC DEVELOPMENT:

Mobile Harbor: U.S. ports are expected to spend $50 billion in port improvements by 2021.

The maritime industry is heading toward larger vessels because of economies of scale. Currently, 42 percent of ship orders are for vessels exceeding 12,000 TEU (20 ft. equivalent container units). None of the US ports are capable of handling more than 14,500 TEU ships on a regular basis which means loss of business and increased cost of imported goods leading to a slower economy. We have recently experienced a shortage in the supply chain around the world.

Mobile Harbor (MH) offers a promising solution in lieu of conventional thinking of increasing the size of the harbor or dredging rivers or raising bridges. Equipped with an "automatic docking system" and "stabilized crane," it can be built 20-30 miles out in the ocean and can attach to any mega container size vessel. It can simultaneously call on one to six mega ships and can cater to the existing ports as a hub, thereby creating jobs and keeping the existing American ports pertinent. Mobile Harbor would also allow offshore custom inspections, keep the coastal marine ecosystem intact, and would provide a good support system to the Coast Guards for open sea rescue operations. The foundation team traveled to the Netherlands and Belgium to forge partnerships in Europe and Africa to deploy this technology which has generated great deal of interest across the world. We propose a percentage of the revenue generation from this project to go toward student loan forgiveness in respective states.

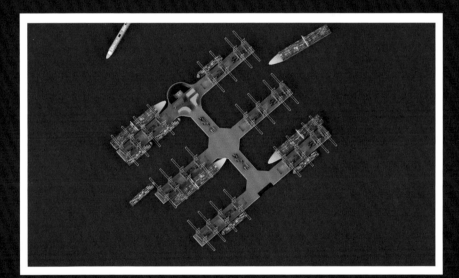

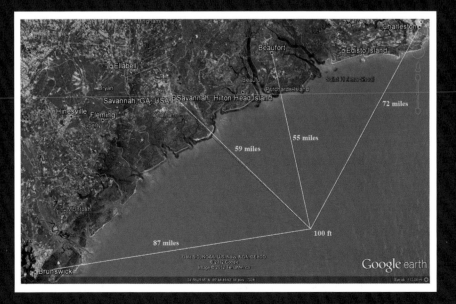

MISSISSIPPI RIVER Business Enterprise Zone:
The Mississippi River is 2,320 miles long.

It passes through or borders Minnesota, Wisconsin, Iowa, Illinois, Missouri, Kentucky, Tennessee, Arkansas, Mississippi, and Louisiana and drains in all or parts of 31 states. Regular floods lead to billions of dollars in business and property losses and recurring relocations of thousands of residents. Fertilizer runoff from farms and animal waste from livestock operations have devoid much of the region of clean drinking water. Furthermore, the lock and dam system that is the backbone of Mississippi transportation infrastructure has not been upgraded since the 1930s and the total estimated cost to overhaul the system is around $125 billion.

The foundation has proposed to create the Mississippi River Business Enterprise Zone to solve the problems of flooding and create business opportunities in the central United State. This solution calls for designating one mile on both sides of the Mississippi River along its complete length as a business enterprise zone and creating a one trillion-dollar Mississippi River Enterprise Development Fund issuing AAA-rated bonds to attract global investment from leading government agencies, private corporations and high net worth individuals. More than $125 billion could be generated and utilized to overhaul the locks and dams and the rest of the funding could be utilized for creation of riverfront civic recreation, generation of hydro-electricity, creation of manufacturing centers of global auto companies, heavy industries, agriculture products, and many other projects. A consortium of companies would be assembled to create the first and largest aquatic enterprise zone utilizing the minds and ideas of people who live along the waterway while integrating a comprehensive water resource utilization plan to keep in mind the environmental concerns and individual States' needs. This project would create hundreds of thousands of jobs in the region with tremendous impact on the economy in the United States.

Above: Unveiling of Andrew Young Statue, funded in part by R. Charles Loudermilk Sr. to celebrate the lifelong achievements of Andrew Young. (*l to r*) Jesse Hill, R. Charles Loudermilk, John Portman, Mayor Shirley Franklin Ambassador Andrew Young and Representative John Lewis. Johnpaul Harris sculpted the statue, April 2008.

Below: Unveiling of street sign for Andrew Young International Boulevard in Atlanta, Georgia.

Above: Andrew and Carolyn Young on their wedding day in Cape Town, South Africa, on March 28, 1996.

Right: Andrew and Carolyn Young celebrating their twenty-fifth wedding anniversary on March 28, 2021.

Carolyn

"YOU ALL NEED TO GET MARRIED IN SOUTH AFRICA"

When Jean got cancer, she realized she wasn't going to make it. Jean and Carolyn were good friends. Whenever Jean's sisters and brothers came and we didn't have room for anybody else in our house, Carolyn would take them to her house. And when we'd leave town to go someplace, and we couldn't take our son Bo, he'd stay with Carolyn.

Jean didn't want me playing around with people. Everybody always thinks that I'm innocent and naive and vulnerable and gullible and so they gotta protect me. Jean was always trying to protect me from wild wild women. She knew Carolyn was not a wild, wild woman. The sicker Jean got, the closer she and Carolyn got.

Now this is a true story. The ambassador from South Africa came to visit Atlanta and I was showing him around. We went out to Lenox Square and drove around Buckhead. We were coming back down Peachtree. And he said, you know, this is a much more cosmopolitan city than I imagined. I said yeah, we got everybody here. I told him that there was an elementary school in the next couple of blocks where they

speak thirty-four languages and classes would be letting out soon, so let's drive by. I pulled around there and whose class was coming out? Carolyn's.

I asked her to come over and meet the South African ambassador. I introduced them and she asked if she could get a ride home. We hadn't gone two blocks when the ambassador said, "You all need to get married in South Africa." And he went on talking about how South Africa was the most beautiful place in the world.

He said, right at the foot of Table Mountain is the American Embassy. And the backyard of the embassy is one of the most beautiful flower

gardens in the world and that would be the perfect place to get married. I didn't say anything. I was embarrassed, because we hadn't gotten to that point where we were even dating. I'm just giving her a ride home. And this man is talking about marriage.

He went back home and he told the U.S. ambassador, who was a friend of mine; his wife of thirty-three years had died of cancer. He was in Washington and he was kind of a playboy and he started dating a lot of women. He called me and asked if I had been dating anybody? It had only been a year since Jean died, and I was working on the Olympics. I didn't have time to date. He asked me who was the woman I had given a ride to? I told him and he said, "You are coming to South Africa in about a month for a meeting, aren't you? You need to bring her and marry her."

And then he went to Adelaide Tambo, whose husband ran the African National Congress while Nelson Mandela was in jail. The last person Jean visited when she was in South Africa, before she died, was Adelaide Tambo. Adelaide, who was about seventy-five and a good African mama, called and asked, "Andy, who is the woman you are about to marry? She cannot get married in an American dress. She has to have an African dress. What's her name? Give me her phone number."

Adelaide calls Carolyn and tells her not to bring an American dress to South Africa if she was going to get married there. And just like that, they plan on a wedding. Two weeks later we leave for South Africa. We just had time for her to get a passport.

And we had our wedding.

The World Traveler

DURING THEIR VISIT TO INDIA,

they were invited by the then Prime Minister Indira Gandhi to her residence. At the time they reached the house, she had just returned from countrywide campaigning and had no helpers at home. Ms. Gandhi asked them to sit in the living room while she went to the kitchen and put on an apron to prepare dinner. Coretta followed her and both of them cooked together and served us dinner. That's an example of humility from two of the strongest women in the world at that time.

Left: Andrew Young and Coretta Scott King during a 1969 trip to India.

Right: Andrew Young sits with Coretta Scott King and King family friend Benita Bennett in front of the Taj Mahal in 1969.

In January 1969, Andrew Young and Coretta Scott King led a delegation to India, where they visited the Taj Mahal and met with political and religious leaders. Mrs. King, who had toured India in 1959 with her husband, Martin Luther King Jr., also spoke to students from the U.S. embassy school in New Delhi.

IT HAS BEEN MY PRIVILEGE TO KNOW AND WORK WITH ANDREW J. YOUNG JR. FOR MORE THAN FIFTY YEARS. OUR FRIENDSHIP HAS BEEN MORE LIKE THAT OF BROTHERS.

Andy's accomplishments throughout his life have positively impacted the lives of millions of people, not only in the South, in Atlanta, and in the United States, but throughout the world. His many careers in leadership positions in every part of his life, in civil and human rights, in the U.S. Congress, as the U.S. Ambassador to the United Nations, as mayor of the City of Atlanta, as an ordained minister, as co-chair of the committee that brought the Centennial Olympic Games to Atlanta, as leader of an organization that brought financial success and stability to numerous developing countries, and in finally establishing with his wife, Carolyn, the Andrew Young Foundation.

Any one of these positions or undertakings would normally have been a lifetime career, but Andy has done them all, mostly to the benefit of others.

Underlying what he has done in service to *all* of us, or better, *overarching* all of these accomplishments is a *very spiritual person*. A person who looks to a higher power to direct his life. He quotes the Bible often, specifically Matthew 25.

The Lord tells His disciples; when I was hungry you fed Me, when I was thirsty you gave Me water, when I was a stranger you invited Me in, when I was naked you clothed Me, when I was in prison you visited Me.
And His disciples asked, "Lord when did we do these things for you?" and He answered, "Verily I say unto you, Inasmuch as ye have done it unto one of the least of these my brethren, ye have done it unto Me."

In 1993, my wife, Sally, and I were living in Eastern Germany, doing work in Eastern Europe. Andy was working for a major engineering firm, Law Engineering, headquartered in Atlanta. He was visiting the mayor of Berlin on some projects. We picked him up at the Berlin Rathaus and traveled to our home in Magdeburg.

The next day we visited the City of Wittenberg—the Minister of Finance and Economy of the state in which we lived arranged with the Wittenberg mayor for a red carpet tour of the city. We were in the Old Town, a well-preserved part of the city where Martin Luther lived in the first half of the sixteenth century. We visited Luther's home, which is now a museum, the City Church where Luther preached, and on to the Castle Church where he nailed the Ninety-five Theses to the church door. This act marked the beginning of the Reformation in 1517. Wittenberg is a very spiritual and inspirational town.

We walked the same cobblestone street, Collegian Strasse, that Martin Luther walked on in the sixteenth century. The same street the Martin Luther King Sr. walked in the 1930s when he decided to change his name and his five-year-old son's name to Martin Luther King Sr. and Martin Luther King Jr.

As we walked we observed the tour buses stopping at Luther's house, then the City Church, and the Castle Church. Tourists would rush in, take a photograph and rush back to their buses, only stopping to buy T-shirts, beer steins, and coffee mugs before leaving immediately for Leipzig.

I said to Andy, "There was so much more that needs to happen here than stopping for one hour between Berlin and Leipzig."

Andy looked up in an instant and said, "There needs to be another Reformation. But this needs to be an Economic Reformation for all of God's children on the entire globe." From that moment, the Wittenberg Center for Global Ethics (WCGE) was formed.

Over the next four years, the work of Andy Young and three other American and German leaders from government and industry was to found and launch the WCGE. Included in this group was Hans Dietrich Genscher, the former Foreign Minister of Germany, with whom Andy had worked to help decolonized African countries when he was the UN Ambassador.

The founding Congress of the Wittenberg Center for Global Ethics was held in 1999 in Wittenberg with more than two hundred world leaders in attendance. The Vision Statement created by the founding group, headed by Young and Genscher, was presented at the Congress. It included the following quotes:

"The Center will identify common core ethical principles that enable people of diverse cultures to grow and develop in one world at peace."

"The Center will find common ground for peaceful coexistence for growth and development based on honesty, integrity, fairness and common good."

"Economic growth for one group must not occur at the expense of other people. A common strategy that leads to absence of fear and hate between peoples, nations and races will be developed. The Center will develop a spirit of sharing the one planet where we live together in peace."

Thank you, Lord, for the work of your servant, Andrew Jackson Young Jr.

Paul Rosser

Andrew Young

»Human Rights and Economic Ethics - The Emerging Markets at the Turn of the 21st Century«

...ndet / Andrew Young will daraus eine Stiftung machen

...n in Atlanta: „Am ...wir nur die Idee"

Wittenbergs OB Eckhard Naumann, der ehemalige UN-Botschafter der USA Andrew Young, der Unternehmer Paul Rosser und Wirtschaftsminister Klaus Schucht in Wittenberg (v. l.).
Foto: B. Forstenbacher

WITTENBERG CENTER FOR GLOBAL ETHICS

Founding Congress

Wittenberg Center for Global Ethics

6th-8th November 1999
Lutherstadt Wittenberg

LEADER SHARES INSPIRATIONAL MESSAGE

JASON FISCHER/News-Press

Former Atlanta mayor Andrew Young speaks to an audience of about 1,300 Friday during the 20th Mayor's Community Prayer Breakfast at the Harborside Convention Hall. Fort Myers Mayor Wilbur Smith, next to the podium, listens.

Young practices, preaches power of prayer

By BETTY PARKER
News-Press staff writer

Family

FOR ALL THAT ANDREW YOUNG has done and seen, nothing is more important to him than his family. He was born the eldest son of Andrew Jackson Young, a dentist, and Daisy Fuller Young, a schoolteacher in New Orleans. Young grew up with his brother, Walter.

He married educator Jean Childs in 1954. Their forty-year union produced four children, Andrea Young, Lisa Alston, Paula Shelton, and Andrew Young III.

"Nothing gives him greater pleasure than a graduation, wedding, christening, or holiday dinner when we are all together," said Andrea Young.

And there is a lot of all of that. Young also has nine grandchildren: Taylor Stanley Iyoho; Kemet and Lena Alston; Caleb, Joshua, and Noah Shelton; and Abigail, Andrew IV, and Amelia Young; and one great-grandchild, Amari Kathryn Iyoho.

Where He leads me, I will follow

I'VE ALWAYS FELT THAT EVERYTHING I'VE DONE HAS BEEN BLESSED BY FORCES BEYOND MY CONTROL.

It's not that I'm that smart, and it's not that I'm that lucky—I'm blessed. And all the crazy things I've touched somehow have worked out.

The best thing that happened to me was that I left the UN when I did. If I had waited another year, I wouldn't have become mayor of Atlanta. We might not have had the Olympics.

Going back to that first climbing to the top of the mountain: there's something that you can do that nobody else can do. There was nobody else. I came down here to work with Martin Luther King, but I really wasn't working with Martin Luther King.

I ended up in an office across the hall from him and his secretary ended up asking me to help with his mail. The next thing I know I am researching his speeches. It just happened. Sam Massell let me negotiate the strikes. Jimmy Carter sent me to the UN. Charlie Loudermilk helped me get elected mayor.

I have lived a blessed life, and I don't know what I did to deserve it, but I've never turned down an opportunity to serve.

Deciding to go to Marion, Alabama, which I'd never heard of, instead of New York and the Olympics, was a real test. That was my first decision of faith. But when I moved to Marion and met the love of my life for the next forty-five years, I figured the Lord knows what he's doing with me. I am reminded of the song we sing in church, "Where He leads me, I will follow." I'll go with Him all the way.

Love for All Mankind: Civil Rights Icon, Congressman, Ambassador, Mayor and Philanthropist Andrew Young shines the shoes of Muhammad Ali.

WHAT IS THE
COMPLETE LIFE?

LENGTH
TO LIVE FOR A PURPOSE BORN

BREADTH
TO BE A PERSON FOR OTHERS

HEIGHT
TO KNOW GOD

DR. MARTIN LUTHER KING, JR.

THE JOURNEY REQUIRES:
HUMILITY – PATIENCE – JOY
COURAGE – FORGIVENESS